The
Hand
on the
Mirror

The Hand on the Mirror

A TRUE STORY OF LIFE BEYOND DEATH

JANIS HEAPHY DURHAM

GRAND CENTRAL
PUBLISHING

NEW YORK   BOSTON

Excerpt from *The Little Prince*, Antoine de Saint-Exupéry. Houghton Mifflin Harcourt, 1943.

All photos courtesy of the author.

Grand Central Publishing
Hachette Book Group
1290 Avenue of the Americas
New York, NY 10104

www.HachetteBookGroup.com

Printed in the United States of America

RRD-C

First Edition: April 2015
10 9 8 7 6 5 4 3 2 1

Grand Central Publishing is a division of Hachette Book Group, Inc. The Grand Central Publishing name and logo is a trademark of Hachette Book Group, Inc.

The Hachette Speakers Bureau provides a wide range of authors for speaking events. To find out more, go to www.hachettespeakersbureau.com or call (866) 376-6591.

The publisher is not responsible for websites (or their content) that are not owned by the publisher.

Library of Congress Cataloging-in-Publication Data has been applied for.

ISBN 978-1-4555-3130-1 (hardcover)
ISBN 978-1-4555-8950-0 (large print)

For Max

Contents

Contents

To love another person is to see the face of God.

Victor Hugo
Les Misérables, 1862

Introduction

This is a story of an unusual personal journey. It's not what you would expect from someone with my traditional upbringing and experience in the hard-edged world of newspapers. It begins with the untimely death of my beloved husband Max Besler in 2004 and follows with a series of extraordinary events that startled me at first, and then intrigued me. Unfolding over eight years, this is a story of my spiritual growth and how my mind gradually opened to realities that I previously would have considered unimaginable. It's a story about love and how love ties us all together in a far more fascinating universe than I ever imagined. In the end, I hope my story will be a source of strength to all who are touched by death, which, of course, is everyone.

The question of what happens after we die has always challenged us. The topic makes us uneasy. Here we are, living active and full lives. Why do we even want to think about death? Then it strikes. We lose someone we love and we are faced with contemplating death and the afterlife. Scientists, theologians, writers, musicians, poets, and artists have all addressed the question directly or indirectly. It is at the core of organized religion's belief system, one that I grew up with as a Presbyterian. We believe that when you die you go to heaven. But what exactly is heaven?

If we knew, not just from the faith of our religions, but from modern science, that our consciousness survives after death, it would profoundly affect how we behave. I think it's arguable that this question of whether or not there is an afterlife is the most important question in life. What could be more important? *The Hand on the Mirror* suggests that we continue on in another form after we die. Simply put, life does not end with our physical death. My hope is to open readers' thinking to this possibility.

The most compelling motivation for writing *The Hand on the Mirror* was the potential to encourage people to talk openly about their experiences of communicating with a loved one after the loved one has passed. I also hope this book will provide readers with not only an emotional framework but also an intellectual foundation of legitimacy for those conversations. These discussions should be out in the open, free of constraint. As a society we could benefit from eliminating the stigma associated with sharing personal stories about the afterlife, including those that involve the supernatural, as mine do.

Fear of embarrassment was a significant part of my reluctance over the years to write this book. I knew that what I revealed would be provocative, and I obsessed over what my family and friends would think. Of course, I knew they loved me, but I was worried that wouldn't stop them from thinking that my profound grief had affected my judgment. And I was also concerned about my wider circle of friends and associates, particularly those I worked with. I was convinced that the bizarre nature of the events I experienced would be impossible for many of these fact-based personalities to accept. Who could blame them? The story is incredible, out of bounds of the normal. And even though there are documenting photographs, people often believe only what they choose to believe, not what may be unbelievable but true.

I know I'm not alone in this fear of being judged. As part of my research, I shared my story and the accompanying photographs with a number of people, and many related to me their experiences with otherworldly events. In fact, they were eager to tell me their stories and sometimes added that they had never shared them with anyone else, in certain cases even their spouses, for fear of how they would be viewed. Learning about their reluctance fueled my courage to come forward.

Most stories have characters, and this one is no exception. You will meet my family, my friends, professors, researchers, psychologists, physicists, spiritual practitioners, and mediums, and a host of other individuals who were part of the journey and pivotal in my investigation. You may be surprised at their similarities of thought, although they are not always expressed with the same language. You will meet a number of key scientific leaders in this field and hear their frustrations in trying to further their exploration. I hope you will come to know them as I have—as fascinating people.

Some technical issues go well beyond my expertise, but I've tried to describe scientific principles and progress in a way that the average reader can understand. My goal in this is to help the scientists and their work get the widespread attention they deserve.

Lasting change is not driven from the top down but from a bottom-up approach. People get behind an idea, and unbelievable things can happen. Abraham Lincoln said it well: "With

public sentiment, nothing can fail; without it nothing can succeed." If readers can feel safe to share their stories about the
survival of consciousness and an afterlife, momentum will build.
That will help drive the topic further into the mainstream,
perhaps leading to more extensive, accurate, and serious media
coverage. With momentum, scientists can explore this field in
a properly funded, more open environment. Any contribution
this book can make to that momentum will be immensely
gratifying to me.

An expanding acceptance of the survival of consciousness
and, therefore, life after death has the potential to bring about
change in all of us. We'll live our lives with more emphasis on
love and less on fear of loss. And maybe, just maybe, we'll begin
to understand our purpose.

Janis Heaphy Durham

It is much easier to recognize error than to find truth;
for error lies on the surface and may be overcome; but
truth lies in the depths, and to search for it is not given
to every one.

Johann Wolfgang von Goethe
1749–1832

the
Hand
on the
Mirror

CHAPTER 1

The Hand on the Mirror

On Sunday, May 8, 2005, my reality changed. That was the day I discovered a large handprint on the mirror of a bathroom in my home in Sacramento, California. It was not an ordinary handprint. Seemingly made of a soft, white, powdery substance, it showed all the facets of the bone structure, as if it were an X-ray. Looking closer, I could see it was the hand of a man because of the masculine shape of the fingers and the wide base of the palm. The handprint stood alone, the image affixed to the mirror and perfectly formed. It had appeared out of nowhere. Literally, nowhere.

The day the hand appeared was the first anniversary of the death of my husband, Max Besler. Max had died in the living room of our home surrounded by family and friends. We had been married for four years when he was diagnosed at the age of fifty-six with esophageal cancer. Six months later, he was gone, devastating my fourteen-year-old son, Tanner, and me. We both loved Max very much, and the three of us had blossomed as a family. On this Mother's Day Sunday a year later, I was still working through my grief and was concerned about how Tanner was coping with his own sorrow. He was so young and impressionable, and like most young men at that age, he wasn't a big talker. I felt pensive and alert on this one-year anniversary, vigilant in my role as mother and protector.

Tanner and I were sitting together at a small table in our backyard in the early afternoon sun. Tanner split his time between our home in Sacramento and his dad's home in El Dorado Hills, about thirty minutes away. Divorce is never easy, but his dad, Bob Heaphy, and I were committed to keeping Tanner's interests first and foremost in our lives. We had worked hard to provide a steady, dependable schedule for him and assurance in deeds and words that even though he lived in two homes, he was loved and supported fully in both. Max had added to that love. On this significant day, I was comforted to have Tanner, with his short-cropped blond hair and athletic physique, next to me. I loved watching him concentrate on his homework, and I smiled a mother's smile as I noticed his habit of moving his lips while he silently read. I was catching up on my own self-imposed homework—the backlog of reading I faced each weekend in my job. After a while, we decided we were hungry, and I got up from the table to go inside and bring us a snack. Tanner was eating like any healthy teenage boy, meaning nonstop. Besides, the food offered a distraction from the sadness in our hearts on this anniversary.

Our home was designed in a U shape, with the master bedroom suite, Tanner's bedroom, and a den on the left side of the U, and the living room, dining room, and library at the center. On the right side of the U were our kitchen, a guest bedroom suite, a laundry room, and the exit to the garage. Max had spent the last month of his life in the guest bedroom instead of our master bedroom because he was more comfortable in a bed by himself, as he was in grave pain. And he insisted I get my sleep since I was working.

Before entering the kitchen to make our snack, I stopped in the bathroom in the guest bedroom suite. That was when I saw the handprint. I knew it was fresh because it hadn't been there when I had combed my hair in front of that mirror an hour earlier. Stunned by the sight, I stood frozen for at least a full minute. I could make no sense of what I saw. At fifty-three years old, I had never experienced anything so completely out of the human realm as this handprint. My eyes were fixed on something unexplainable. My brain was working to catch up with my eyes. Was I losing my mind? Maybe. Had someone snuck into the house to play a trick? Doubtful.

Tanner and I would have seen or heard anyone through the open patio doors. How could a human hand show the transparency of an X-ray? Slowly, my voice started to function, and I managed to shout out the words, "Tanner, come here. Quickly! Hurry!"

"Mom, what's wrong? Are you okay?" he asked.

"Look," I cried out. "You didn't do this, did you?" I was sounding somewhat hysterical to myself at this point.

I knew as soon as the words left my lips that he hadn't made the handprint because he'd been sitting next to me throughout the time we worked together and during the hour since I'd visited the bathroom. Just to double-check, I asked Tanner to hold his right hand up next to the powdery right hand print to see how it compared. I realized how ludicrous it was to think he had made the print. The image was much larger than his hand and shaped differently.

We both stared at the handprint, speechless and awestruck. Slowly we turned from the image to face each other. Our eyes locked. We knew we were witnessing something astounding, and we were a bit frightened. It was just so strange; we had no idea what it was. Our minds could not comprehend what our eyes were telling us.

"Mom, I don't get it. What is that?" Tanner asked, turning his eyes back to the mirror.

I thought as carefully as I could before answering him. Reacting dramatically wouldn't serve either one of us. My maternal instincts kicked in, and I resolved to calm down. I wanted to sound stable and set a good example for him. Children read us more clearly than we often realize, I had learned, and overreacting wasn't helpful to him—or me, for that matter. But I also knew I had to be honest, and pretending it wasn't extraordinary was disingenuous.

"I'm not sure what it is, Tanner."

Then I ventured a question of my own: "Do you think there's any relationship to Max since it's the first anniversary of his death?" I knew he loved Max, so he wouldn't be frightened by the question. I also knew it wasn't the first time we had witnessed something strange after Max died, but nothing had been remotely close to the shocking nature of this handprint.

"Maybe, but how weird is that? And how could he make it happen if he's gone, Mom?" Tanner asked.

Of course, I had no answer, only a sense that I needed to remain calm and inquisitive but not emotional. "I guess for now we don't know, Tanner. Why don't you take a break and go out to the driveway and shoot some baskets?"

"Okay, Mom, but call me if you need me," he said, sounding very grown-up.

4

I gave him a hug and told him I'd join him outside in a few minutes. I grabbed my camera and took several photographs. I didn't know what this image was, but I did know I had to document it. I should have done more, like get a sample of the powdery substance for analysis or have a forensic examination conducted of the fingerprints. But I was so stunned, it just didn't occur to me.

What did occur to me was the implication of the timing of the handprint. It showed up on the exact date of Max's death, immediately raising the question of whether Max was reaching out to me. Like most wives, I could recall precisely what my husband's hands looked like. The wide palm print on the mirror, juxtaposed with the long, narrow fingers, was reminiscent of the shape of Max's hands.

I didn't have an explanation for the phenomenon, but it certainly didn't fit neatly with the traditions I had been schooled in growing up. As a child, I had been heavily influenced by my father, a Presbyterian minister deeply devoted to God and his faith. But like many people, I had evolved in my thinking as I grew older. Now my faith was not as central to my daily life, so I didn't have a tidy solution for thinking how this handprint might relate to heaven or an afterlife. What I did know was that I was experiencing an entirely foreign dimension. I was baffled by the mystery.

I had to ask myself, could this be a paranormal event? Was this a ghost? Because Max had died in our home, had a part of him remained? Was he visiting me to let me know there was more? Had he figured out a method for contacting me that was nothing short of miraculous? I've always been open in life, and I wanted to be open now. But I was scared, too. Entering the unknown was intimidating.

From a practical standpoint, I didn't have time to be distracted and frightened. Instead, I compartmentalized the remarkable event, setting it aside for further thought when I could attend to it. After all, I had a son to raise and a job to do. I was overwhelmed with surviving my grief. My life had been ripped apart by Max's death, and it was all I could do to function in my roles as mother and newspaper executive. I cherished those roles. They were what fulfilled me. Succeeding at them was imperative. I could not fail.

My upbringing influenced me, as well, in setting the event aside. My father's role as a minister meant he was a prominent figure in our community. We were taught as children that our personal behavior represented not just ourselves but our family and, by extension, Dad's public position. We were expected to behave accordingly and not draw outside the lines of convention. That example stuck with me as an adult.

Now as publisher and president of *The Sacramento Bee*, in the state capital of California, I was a public figure myself. Our publication was influential not only locally but also statewide and nationally as the flagship of the McClatchy Company newspaper chain. When I was being recruited, I remember a McClatchy executive asking me, "Are you comfortable with lots of public attention?" It wasn't until I was further along in the job that I came to understand the wisdom of that question. My life was naturally under the microscope, and I wasn't about to foster any criticism that could emanate from disclosing such a strange event. So I kept it private.

Not knowing what to do with the handprint after discovering it, I just left it on the mirror until Wednesday, when my housekeeper, Helen Dennis, came to clean on her regular day. Helen had been close to Max and was an enormous help when

Max was going through his cancer treatments. He and I trusted her and viewed her as family. She was discreet with the details of Max's illness and protected both his privacy and his dignity when he was ill. I walked her into the bathroom before I left for work to show the image to her. I was curious how she'd respond. She was astounded but calm as we stared at the mirror together. We both wondered if this was a sign from Max since it was tied to the anniversary of his death. After a few minutes, I knew I had to get on with my day, so I told her it was okay to go ahead and clean the mirror. I saw no reason to keep it longer than the three days it had been there. Helen later told me that Windex removed the image, but she had to scrub.

So I marched forward in my life. But in my determination to carry on, I could not escape the thought of the curious mystery I had discovered on the bathroom mirror. It was a powerful image that left an indelible imprint on my mind.

CHAPTER 2

Family Matters

My father had an immense impact on me as I was growing up. He was the primary influence in my life. An extraordinary man, he was self-made in every respect.

His mother was Agnes Olson, born Agnes Anderson on April 16, 1884, in Skåne, Sweden. On the day before her twelfth birthday, she sailed alone to America from Göteborg, Sweden, on a ticket purchased by her mother. Though our family history doesn't give us the specifics of why Agnes came to America, we believe she left Sweden for improved economic opportunity, as was the case for many young Swedes immigrating to the United States during the nineteenth century. But Agnes was exceptionally young to travel so far alone under the terrible conditions in steerage aboard a ship. When Agnes arrived, she lived with a distant aunt in Brooklyn, New York, where she cleaned houses to support herself and sent money back home to her family.

At sixteen she returned to Sweden. Then she sailed back to

America a second time by herself when she was eighteen. Ten years later she returned to Sweden and shortly thereafter married Axel Wilhelm Olson in January 1912.

A soldier with the Swedish cavalry, Axel received a land homestead in America as payment for his service. Agnes and Axel decided to begin their new life together in Ong, Nebraska, where other Swedes were living. Having little money or resources, they booked their tickets in third class on a ship leaving from England. But travel from Sweden to the port in Southampton, England, was tenuous, much of it on horseback. They arrived late and missed the ship they had booked. The ship was the *Titanic*.

When Grandpa Axel and Grandma Agnes finally arrived in Clay County, Nebraska, the prairies still had bison, wolf, antelope, and buffalo. John Frémont, known as "the Pathfinder," had explored the area as he searched for a shorter route to the West, and the first homesteaders arrived in 1857. Now, Grandpa and Grandma were raising their family in this rugged terrain. It was a hard life. By the mid-1930s, between the Great Depression and the Dust Bowl drought, only the hardiest remained. But Grandpa scratched out a living as a carpenter, and Grandma raised six children.

They placed a strong emphasis on faith in God and insisted that education was the key to their new life in America, where anything was possible. All of the children graduated from college. The family focus on faith and learning undoubtedly influenced my father to believe, as he put it, that he had a calling to be a minister. After marrying my mother and graduating from college, he went on to earn a master's degree from Union Theological Seminary in New York in 1946.

He often spoke of those days at Union, where he felt privileged to study under some of the great theologians of the 1950s.

Reinhold Niebuhr and Paul Tillich were his professors, and Henry Sloane Coffin was president emeritus. Dad was proud of his education, and he never lost his love of theology and his deep devotion to God.

What I learned about heaven I learned from my dad and our church. The Presbyterian faith I inherited is that when you die, your soul goes to be with God. Beyond Sunday school, the sermons, and the reading, many talks with my father helped form my early conception of heaven, or an afterlife.

One conversation in particular sticks out in my memory. It must have been around 1960, when I was nine or ten years old. Dad and I were walking downtown in Hamilton, Ohio, where we lived. It was a community of seventy-five thousand near Cincinnati in southern Ohio. We were on a narrow side street next to the Front Street Presbyterian Church, where he served as the minister. We were probably headed to a church class or choir practice. I vividly remember touching his hand and asking him to stop and lean down to talk to me. I had a question. It was not whether there was a heaven, but where was heaven? He recited John 14:1–2: "Let not your heart be troubled: ye believe in God, believe also in me. In my Father's house are many mansions: if it were not so, I would have told you. I go to prepare a place for you."

Then he stood still and talked to me eye to eye. He gave me the example of our family and the love we have in our own home here on earth. He said it was like that in heaven. And he told me that just as he and my mother would never desert me or stop loving me, so God in heaven is the same. God, too, has a home and a safe place for all of us to be one day. And he ended our little talk by telling me that God is infinite, living with us and within us, not only here but in heaven when we die.

As I reflect on it now I am struck by how hard my dad worked when he was in his prime. He was tireless and committed, his days filled with hospital visits, sermons, weddings, and funerals. But more important was his all-encompassing faith in and devotion to God. I would often hear him praying quietly alone late at night, and I listened closely to hear the soothing whisper of his words, not really understanding everything but feeling a sense of reverence that resonates with me to this day.

My father taught me something else that has remained with me for a lifetime—that there is no compromising on truth. In my eyes, he was the living definition of strong character, and he often said, "Character is destiny." Clearly possessed of his Swedish mother's independence, he encouraged me to question and examine so I could form my own opinions. "You have to do the right thing, no matter how difficult," he told me.

Looking back on it, I have come to believe that my childhood and adolescence was a period where I put authority first. And I, like a lot of us in the Midwest in the 1950s, did it willingly. In my case, my dad was a dual authority figure—my father and my minister.

In the ensuing years I gradually learned that faith is far more complicated than just "believing." I owe that to my dad, as well. Like many people, I wanted to dig beneath the surface to ask more questions. By the second phase of my life, say, ages twenty-one to fifty, I was in pursuit of a more meaningful spiritual life just as I was pursuing a meaningful life in every respect. While I was grateful for the religious values I'd received at home and in church, I still found myself searching. I was inquisitive and curious, looking for an intellectual and philosophical framework as much as religious stimulation.

Dad again was a great resource. When I was forty-four, he

recommended a list of books. While many were abstract, they launched my spiritual expedition into other realms. These books went beyond my classic Christian upbringing and challenged me to think more broadly:

Man's Search for Meaning by Viktor E. Frankl
Escape from Freedom and *The Sane Society* by
    Erich Fromm
Man Against Himself by Karl A. Menninger
Man, the Unknown by Alexis Carrel
Man's Search for Himself and *Love and Will* by Rollo May
On Being a Real Person by Harry Emerson Fosdick
Reverence for Life by Albert Schweitzer
Spirit and Reality by Nicolas Berdyaev
The Higher Happiness by Ralph W. Sockman
The Courage to Be by Paul Tillich
The Nature and Destiny of Man by Reinhold Niebuhr

I dove in and read and read. Some of the reading was beyond me. But the more I read, the more I began opening up to the idea that there was—yes, more. The exposure didn't reduce my faith in God. It enhanced it. I was lucky because I wasn't afraid to wander off the path and satisfy my curiosity. It was Dad who had said, "I'd rather have you search and challenge your faith than blindly follow."

While my dad played such an influential role in my religious and spiritual development and evolution, my mother was a different story. We never really got along, and our relationship was often upsetting. It was a classic personality clash. Perhaps it's not that unusual for mothers and daughters to have difficult relationships. I know many women who have told me about similar conflicts with their mothers. And interestingly, I often end up in close friendships with these women.

It started when I was young. My mother irritated me, and I imagine I irritated her. I don't know why. I often thought maybe she didn't like me because I was a girl instead of a boy. She practically worshipped my brothers. Or maybe it was competition or jealousy surrounding Dad. Whatever the reason, in my view, she was just an unpleasant person when it came to me. I'm not saying I didn't deserve some of this treatment. I could have been more mature in our exchanges, but for some reason I often resorted to immature behavior. Over time it became a pattern that persisted throughout our lives. This wasn't about love. I loved her, and I know she loved me. Maybe it was a power struggle.

I could write an entire book of stories involving my mother and me. One Thanksgiving when I was in my thirties, my parents came to visit. I had been working for *The Los Angeles Times* on the business side in advertising for at least a decade. After dinner, Mom and I were doing dishes and she said, "You know, your brothers have become far more politically conservative than your dad and I raised them to be. We're disappointed they haven't retained our liberal perspective. I think it's because they're in the business world."

I responded, "Well, I'm in the business world, Mom, and that hasn't happened to me."

To which she said, "No, you're not in the business world. You're in advertising."

I was speechless.

Years later when I left *The Los Angeles Times* to join *The Sacramento Bee*, I was telling Mom and Dad about my new job over dinner one night. Running a newspaper was not an insignificant responsibility.

Mom's response: "Don't you think you'll need some training?"

Training? I think maybe twenty-three years constitutes a bit, don't you? I thought.

Instead I just smiled and said, "Pass the peas, please."

Mom was a master of guilt. One of the most hurtful incidents involved Grandpa Thorndike, her father. Harry Thorndike was a quintessential grandfather, and we all loved him. He was funny, smart, and industrious, and he worshipped and loved Ada, our grandmother, as much as I've ever seen anyone love another. He owned a general store in Cambridge, Nebraska, where my mother was raised. Grandpa Thorndike died when I was around thirty years old. Not long after, Mom and Dad came to visit me. We had just seated ourselves for dinner when Mom turned to me and said, "Do you know what I found in Grandpa's desk drawer at their house?"

I said, "No, I don't."

"Well, I found a letter from you where you had said you'd be sending him something by a certain date. He had marked the note 'to come from Janis soon,' and guess what? You didn't send it in time before he died."

I was crushed. Like a helium balloon losing air swiftly, I felt myself falling. Why did she choose to say this to me when she knew how much I loved him and how much this would hurt? And worst of all, I had no ability to change it now. Or so I thought at the moment.

"Pass the potatoes, please," I said.

That night, I dreamed of a long, narrow staircase leading to the third floor of a home. I looked up and saw a brilliant light at the top of the staircase. I followed the light, and holding the railing, I slowly walked up each step until I reached the third floor. I turned left and saw a short hall with several white doors. I walked down the hall and stopped at the first door.

Thumbtacked to the door was a simple index card. On it was a note. It said, "Dear Janis, you don't have to worry about the letter. I know you love me and I love you. Grandpa."

I was born in Kalamazoo, Michigan, in 1951, the third of four children. My brothers, Kurt and Brian, were older, and my sister, Signe, was the youngest. We had a typical upbringing except that in the 1950s we lived in a manse, which is a minister's home next door to the church. Routines ruled, and we were taught the value of hard work and productivity. Dad was busy with his ministry, and Mom presided over our daily lives. Each Sunday began at nine a.m. in Sunday school, and then I sang in the church choir at the eleven a.m. service. (Luckily, no one asks me to sing anymore. That is definitely not one of my strengths.) After our early Sunday dinner at home, we returned to church around six thirty p.m. for youth fellowship classes.

During the week we enjoyed spaghetti dinners in our church hall. In the summer we joined other students for Bible study and summer camp. Attendance at these events was mandatory in our home, and I was quite proud of my "Sunday School Perfect Attendance" pin. I liked the structure, the stability these activities gave me, and, perhaps even more, the opportunity to socialize. I was fortunate to have had this great experience growing up. I learned the value of community and of routine in establishing a religious foundation.

On weekday evenings our family would engage in lively dinner conversations in which all the children were expected to participate. Those meals were noisy, as all of us fought to be heard. We subscribed to both morning and evening newspapers (ah, for the good old days), and Mom and Dad would often quiz us to see if we understood what we had read.

After dinner there was no TV. Ever. Seriously. We were supposed to study, and I did—sort of. But whenever possible I would sneak phone calls to my girlfriends on my beige princess phone with the long cord, whispering in hushed tones about goofy girl stuff. This seemed far more important than studying. I did enough studying to please my parents, but no one would ever label me "top of the class."

The Presbyterian Church placed my father in a number of communities over the course of his career. We moved from Kalamazoo to Maumee, Ohio, near Toledo, and then to Hamilton. Time was marked by the seasons, and I still marvel at the changes each season brings. My favorite was the fall, when we raked leaves and built bonfires at football games. There wasn't a lot of organized entertainment or shopping when I was growing up. We invented our own entertainment. In the winter, we would ice-skate on the creek behind our home.

Each summer our family rented a U-Haul trailer, jammed every conceivable piece of camping equipment into it, and took off for a month, traveling throughout the states in an old Ford station wagon with wood siding. I remember the four of us kids wedged together in the backseat, with the dog behind us, barely able to breathe because it was so hot (air-conditioning in cars was still rare then). We stayed at state parks, and I loved the smell of the campfire as we gathered around it on canvas chairs and told stories. Then we crawled into the tent, which took way too long to put up, sleeping like sardines on air mattresses. In the morning we spent three painful hours breaking the camp down and stuffing the equipment back in the tiny U-Haul.

During my years in junior and senior high school, I continued my bad study habits and became quite proficient at appearing to study while primarily focusing on hanging out with my girlfriends. Piled together in the front and back seats (no worry about seat belts in those days) and with the radio blasting something like "Respect" by Aretha Franklin or "Windy" by The Association, we would cruise through the Big Boy and A&W Root Beer drive-ins after the games. I tried out for cheerleading for six years in a row and miraculously made the squad each time. It wasn't due to any talent. Rather it was an ability to yell loudly and jump around a lot. This was not necessarily an easy thing to pull off because it involved messing up my teased and heavily sprayed beehive hairdo that I took pains to protect. In my sophomore year, the tryouts consisted of doing cheers on the basketball court in front of whoever showed up to fill the bleachers. The "audience" clapped for each cheerleader, and the one who received the loudest, longest claps won the contest. Fortunately, my brother Brian, who closely resembled the Fonz in every respect, brought all his motorcycle buddies to the event. Guess who won?

In my senior year, I was voted onto the homecoming court, which thrilled me to no end. I had literally propelled myself there by relentlessly campaigning for it. And upon graduation, I was awarded not with the title "smartest student" or "most likely to succeed" but with "most naïve." In short, I was consumed by the superficial and hadn't awakened to the real world. Anything with deep consequence was beyond my comprehension.

My perfunctory life changed when I left for Ohio State University in Columbus, Ohio. It was 1969. My parents could not afford to pay my full tuition and room and board. So to help foot the bill, I worked when I wasn't in class. I waited on tables, taught swimming, and sold women's clothing in a boutique. Fortunately, the Nixon administration offered a special loan program for students entering the teaching field, which was my saving grace. I enrolled in the College of Education and determined that one day I would teach in the secondary school system. I made my college payments with borrowed funds. It took me ten years to pay off that loan at $77.50 a month. I had a little payment book, and I can still remember the sound each perforated stub would make as I tore it off and mailed it away with my check.

College transformed me in ways I didn't fully recognize until much later in life. Ohio State University was home to Woody Hayes, the famous football coach. But happy days of football games and cheering against rival Michigan faded by the end of my freshman year with the tragedy that took place just two and a half hours away at Kent State University. On May 4, 1970, Ohio National Guard troops shot and killed four students and wounded nine others during a student rally protesting the Vietnam War and the U.S. bombing campaign in Cambodia.

The protests were not just at Kent State during this tumultuous time. Ohio State University students joined other students at Harvard, Columbia, and Berkeley and across the entire country in demonstrating against the U.S. involvement in the Vietnam War. Governor James A. Rhodes ordered Ohio National Guardsmen onto the Ohio State University campus in an attempt to control student riots. There was chaos, confusion, and tear gas as helicopters flew overhead. Seeing troops on our campus was chilling. Terribly frightened, my roommates and

I ran for shelter in our dorm and ended up stuffing big white towels under the door to our room because the tear gas was burning our eyes.

I would never again be the same naïve person who had walked onto that campus eight months before. My simplistic view of life had been shattered. Ohio State University canceled classes shortly after the Kent State students were killed, and I drove home to Hamilton with friends, confounded and confused. Like many other students during the Vietnam War era, I was grieving not only for the loss of lives in the war but also for the loss of lives on the Kent State campus.

I spent the summer before my sophomore year feeling true anxiety for the first time. Watching tensions on our campus erupt into violence forced me to confront my position on the war, on authority in general, and on what mattered in life. I could feel a shift as I was evolving and maturing. While I had a solid foundation from my upbringing, I wasn't sure I was equipped for the broader world I was experiencing. I felt I was in a transitional space and not certain which direction to go. In the fall, instead of sticking it out at Ohio State University, I chose a safer route and transferred to Miami University in Oxford, Ohio, a smaller, far more conservative environment. Like many college students then and now, I was doing battle with myself over who I was and who I wanted to be.

After graduating from Miami University in 1973, I began teaching junior high English in Seven Mile, Ohio, a small village with a population of 751 people, just seven miles from my hometown of Hamilton (hence the name Seven Mile). I was clinging to the safety net. But I realized that if I wanted to make something of myself, I was going to have to get serious about studying. I completed my master's degree in education from Miami in 1976. I had finally learned that studying pays off.

I had been putting off dealing with a creeping sense of confinement and restraint in my life. Something that was born in me in my college years was growing, and I could no longer ignore it. Eventually I told myself, *Enough of this small-town life. Enough of ordinary and predictable. It's time to move on.* As much as I loved my teaching job and my friends, I wanted exposure to a wider worldview than a tiny town in Ohio could offer. Maybe my grandmother's DNA was stronger than I realized.

One day in the late afternoon I was standing in the Edgewood Junior High School parking lot next to my nifty Mustang, ready to leave for the day, when a fellow faculty member approached me. She had lived in the village her entire life and had returned after college to teach. She told me she had just bought a home of her own in Seven Mile and managed to get a thirty-year loan. She said she was looking forward to spending the rest of her life right there in rural southern Ohio. Then she got in her Volkswagen bug and slowly drove away. *Oh no, that could be me,* I thought as I watched her taillights disappear down the country road. I knew it was time to leave.

Robin Gaylord was my best friend. We'd known each other since we were about seven years old. Our parents were good friends, and her father, Dr. Paul Gaylord, had been our family dentist. Robin and I decided to hit the road together. We picked California as our destination and said good-bye to our families and friends. We figured California was as far as we could go, and we could always come back. We bought army-green pup tents and walkie-talkies that looked like bricks (no cell phones in those days) and followed our KOA (Kampgrounds of America) map from state to state, with Robin driving her yellow Camaro and me following in my blue Mustang, my bicycle strapped to the back. Other than my clothes, books, and bike, I had sold everything, not that I had a lot to sell.

After arriving in Los Angeles in 1976, I quickly focused on finding a job. I loved newspapers, so I decided to apply at *The Los Angeles Times* in downtown L.A. Since I was an English major, I thought I'd start with the news department. That was naïve and didn't work, so I made my way to the business side. I applied multiple times in advertising, but they kept asking if I had any experience other than teaching, which of course I didn't. Then I would reply that if they'd only hire me, I could get some. Despite my failing strategy, I persisted out of stubbornness, if nothing else.

Finally, in what turned out to be my last interview, I decided to pull out the best quarter of my graduate school transcript, which I'd neatly tucked into my purse. I placed it before the interviewer on his massive walnut desk so he could clearly see my straight-A performance, something even I was surprised I had accomplished.

"I was just wondering, does this count for anything?" I asked.

Something about that impetuous act caught his attention, and he rotated his large frame in his comfortable leather chair to affix his eyes dead center on mine. I thought that I'd really blown it. But I was wrong.

He leaned forward and asked, "Where did you grow up? Tell me about your parents."

I couldn't believe it. The tone of the interview had shifted. I saw he genuinely cared. His name was Don Maldonado. A gregarious man who was most definitely in charge, he wielded real power as the director of advertising for *The Los Angeles Times*.

I told him my story. When I mentioned that my father had grown up in Ong, Nebraska, he suddenly interrupted. "You can't be serious. I know that town. Who was your dad?"

I told him my dad was Elvin Olson.

He said, "Don't move. I need to make a quick call."

He picked up the receiver of his black push-button desk phone (this was 1976) and made the call. What I heard Don say was, "You have to come down here right now. Trust me." Then he hung up. In about five minutes, in walked a handsome, glamorous, and elegantly dressed man with a deep tan. He carried himself with aplomb.

"Janis, meet Vance Stickell," said Don.

Vance was the executive vice president of marketing, the most senior position reporting to the publisher, Otis Chandler. Vance extended a warm handshake and sat down with us.

"Janis is interviewing for an entry-level job here in advertising. Guess who her dad is and where he's from, Vance?" asked Don.

"I have no idea," Vance responded politely.

"Tell him, Janis," Don instructed.

"My father is Elvin Olson. He's from Ong, Nebraska."

"Your father is Elvin?" Vance asked with a stunned expression. "That means your grandmother is Agnes Olson. My mother and your grandmother were friends in Ong. I know the entire Olson clan."

He turned to me and asked about my family and how I had arrived at *The Los Angeles Times*. We chatted for a while as Don sat back and observed. Vance was very gracious. Finally,

23

he slowly shifted back in his seat to speak to Don. "Let's hire her," he said. He then stood up, gave me a warm hug, and left the room, having altered my life forever.

What are the chances that two people sitting in an office in Los Angeles County, home to more than 7 million people at the time, would share their ancestry from a farm town of roughly 150 people? (As of the 2010 census, there were 63.)

And yet it happened. This uncanny encounter launched my newspaper career. Had he not been there, I seriously doubt I would have been offered the job. And then what? Where would I have ended up? How would my entire life have unfolded? I don't know, but I believe it was not just fortuitous. Rather, I think it was my first experience with synchronicity. Only I wasn't paying attention because I had no clue what synchronicity was. It would be three decades before I understood.

I stayed for three years, winning "salesman" of the year my third year. (I don't think they had ever made a plaque that wasn't for a man.) Then I was recruited by ABC Publications to work in advertising at *Los Angeles Magazine*, a local publication in Century City. After several years there, I worked for *Omni* magazine, a national publication, for a few more years. I eventually returned to *The Los Angeles Times* with the goal of using what I'd learned and moving into management. It took me eleven years, but I worked my way up the ranks to be named senior vice president of advertising. I was responsible for $800 million in annual revenue (a staggering number relative to today's newspaper industry plight) and some eight hundred employees. We had offices in Los Angeles, San Francisco, Chicago, and New York, so I spent much of my time on the road. To say I was driven is an understatement. I was obsessed. I loved the work, the people, and the culture of the newspaper business.

I felt I had found purpose in my career, that I was working in an industry that mattered.

In late 1997, the McClatchy Company approached me to run its flagship newspaper in Sacramento. Founded more than 140 years earlier, *The Sacramento Bee* had never had a publisher, instead splitting the top executive duties between an editor and a president, who jointly reported to the corporate office. With a consulting firm's advice, McClatchy conducted a nationwide search for a single executive to oversee the entire newspaper, including news and all business functions. I was the chosen candidate. At age forty-six, I accepted the exciting opportunity to drive the financial success of a complicated business with two thousand employees as well as to support the newspaper's practice of strong journalism. And we did. *The Bee* has won five Pulitzer Prizes since 1857, and two of them were awarded during my ten-year tenure. While I am proud of our paper's performance, the credit goes to the individual journalists who won them and to the McClatchy family heritage, one that holds journalistic accuracy and quality at its core. These were the most rewarding and gratifying years of my career. I feel incredibly fortunate to have had the responsibility, and I covet my memories of that precious decade, difficult as the newspaper business became over the ensuing years.

My career offered a great deal of fulfillment, but it was second to my role as a mother. After all, work is what we do. Being a parent is who we are. Tanner was born in 1990 to my husband, Bob, and me. I had been told years earlier that I would never conceive after a serious bout of appendicitis put me in intensive care in the hospital for five days. Bob and I were elated when at the age of thirty-eight, I learned a baby was on the way. The obstetrician referred to Tanner as "his miracle baby."

I have no doubt that Tanner will be happy and do well throughout his life, in part, because he is driven. He has an urgency and purpose about him that has benefited him scholastically and in his career. He has always been highly competitive, particularly as an athlete. In high school he played football, basketball, and rugby. Rugby is a brutal sport. You don't play unless you're fearless and tough—really tough. Unlike football, players wear no pads, helmets, or protective gear. The uniforms are their jerseys and shorts. While running on the field, crashing into each other, and falling into big piles, they utter grunting sounds that remind me of the fighters in *Gladiator*, the movie starring Russell Crowe. (I closed my eyes and prayed during about 90 percent of Tanner's games.) Tanner began playing rugby at age fourteen, and his passion for the game continued at UCLA, where he played on the team all four years.

This competitive drive probably can be traced back to his grandmother, and I hope I have had some kind of positive influence. I've done with him what most of us try to do with our children: set a good example and provide the advice and counsel to help him grow into a well-rounded, fulfilled adult. I am proud of the man he has become.

CHAPTER 3

Max

I came to know Max Besler in the fall of 1999, after moving to Sacramento a year and a half earlier. I was divorced and trying to manage a new job, as well as make sure nine-year-old Tanner was acclimating to his new environment and school. I first heard about Max over lunch with a friend. She said, "He's erudite and a true Renaissance man. He's really smart."

Born in 1948, Max began his life in New York City. Two years later, his family moved west to Orange County, California. Max's father (also named Max) had been an aide to General Omar Bradley during World War II, and once in California, his father edited *The Anaheim Gazette*. Max was an only child from a close family. Sitting with his parents, he listened to music extensively growing up and spent many hours reading with them as well.

He attended California State University, Fullerton, earning undergraduate and graduate degrees. Four years in the air force followed graduation, and then Max went to work for a

California congressman, where a love of politics took deep root. In 1988 he moved to Sacramento to work for a political consulting firm.

Max loved classical music. He came by his talent through DNA, as his mother was an opera singer and concert pianist. He learned to play the trumpet and piano as a child, but his was not to be a life of performing. So he began to collect CD recordings, exclusively of classical music. I think it was the precision and elegance of music that he loved. Max was a precision kind of guy. He demonstrated that by composing his own symphony, a feat few others achieve. His tastes were broad, but he particularly loved Gustav Mahler and the Russian composers. It wasn't enough to have a recording of a certain piece. He owned multiple recordings of the same piece performed by different orchestras or conductors and could distinguish the subtleties between them. He knew every one of his eighteen hundred CDs, which I have since donated to the Community Library in Ketchum, Idaho, an old mining town near better-known Sun Valley, where I live. It's a small town, but the library is well used and supported. Happily, the Max Besler Classical Music Collection is growing and playing a role in the community. Each year, recordings of the pieces performed by the nationally acclaimed Sun Valley Summer Symphony are added to it. "If Max Besler's life were scored as a symphony, the music would be elegant, graceful, alternatively playful and profound, and over far too soon," said the opening paragraph of *The Sacramento Bee's* newspaper article on Max's death.

Max's other great passions were books and wine. He read constantly across a broad spectrum of literature, and his primary goal was to learn. If he was sitting, he was reading. I have known only a handful of people who read a book a week. And his wine collection, like his book collection, was varied and broad. While he was fond of French burgundies and California pinot noirs, he was knowledgeable across a full range of wines.

In addition, Max was a talented professional. As Jeff Raimundo, his best friend and business partner, described him, "Max was a premier political counselor; he could read polls as artfully as he read music."

The more I heard about Max in my early time in Sacramento, the more I hoped our paths would cross, although I had heard he was dating a woman associated with the Crocker Art Museum. Max's friend, and later mine, David Berkley, who owned a high-end specialty wine and food store, described Max this way: "When you walk into his head, you are not going in a straight line. He has a lot of rooms up there." It turned out that a member of our senior management team at the newspaper also knew Max and told me his firm, Townsend Raimundo Besler & Usher, was well respected for its consulting work. I shamelessly started dropping hints to various friends that I would like to meet him. No results. *He must be serious about his Crocker Art Museum girlfriend,* I thought.

I had heard that Max's firm had periodic gatherings, called "salon dinners," at the senior partner's home, where invited guests would discuss politics and local issues. It was a smart way of marketing the firm's services. One day my assistant, Gloria Mejia, said, "Oh, by the way, some guy named Max Besler called and invited you to a salon dinner at a private home. Do you want me to call and give him your regrets?" Her thinking was correct. Given my position at a newspaper, attending a salon dinner of this kind was not customary. However, lunch with him one-on-one was fine. So I told Gloria that I'd make the call, and I did. And that lunch is how it all started.

We met at Biba Restaurant, an authentic Italian restaurant near his office and mine. Both of us came with our professional armor. But by dessert I could tell this was going to be more than a business association. I was delighted. Max was, indeed, erudite and interesting. I wanted to know him better. And he was obviously flirting. Of course, so was I. We began dating, and I found him to be kind, generous, patient, and thoughtful. He was often analytical and introspective. He was extremely smart and, best of all, hilarious. I loved talking with him, and we could talk and walk for hours. He was driven by an insatiable curiosity and passion for life. I think that's why he was such a voracious reader and why he loved collecting wine, art, and classical music. His ability to absorb and retain information was astonishing. I couldn't get enough of him and his mind. We struck up a magical relationship, and I was as happy as I'd ever been. Over time he became my lover, my teacher, and my best friend.

Three months and many dates later, he invited me to Auberge du Soleil, an exclusive resort in Napa, where he'd arranged for a suite with a fireplace and a masseuse for me. Max knew exactly how to treat a woman. That night he told me he loved me. *Well, about time*, I thought. I had been in love with him for a while. Five months later, we were married, on May 20, 2000. I was overjoyed. Max loved not only me but also my son. We were a family.

Tanner remembers Max as easygoing and brilliant. "There was nothing you could ask about anything that he wouldn't know at least something about it." He credits Max for many of the interests and tendencies he has as a young adult. He noted that Max came into his life at an influential time for a boy, and he says losing Max—and seeing my devastation at the loss—was the most difficult thing he has endured. But memories of Max will always bring a smile to Tanner. He used the same word I had used to describe Max: hilarious. "He was always making people laugh."

Max was an accomplished chef, and thankfully he did most of the cooking in our house. It was only natural that a love of great food and wine led Max to Napa Valley. He had been going to Napa for years before I met him, and his dream was to own a home there. Together we made that a reality, eventually buying and remodeling a small house in Yountville. We spent many happy weekends there.

Max filled our Yountville and Sacramento homes with books. He didn't think they were part of the décor. He had read every one of the thousands he owned. He was partial to nonfiction, reading many books about the civil war as well as World Wars I and II. He also loved philosophy. He took a particular interest in books offering historical accounts of religious figures. And he had an intellectual curiosity about the life of Jesus even though he did not practice a formal religion himself. When we first began dating in 1999, Garry Wills, the prolific Pulitzer Prize–winning author, had just published a book on Saint Augustine. I was traveling in New York on business and asked Max if I could bring him anything home as a little gift. The only thing he wanted was that book. That same year I remember him reading Thomas Cahill's *Desire of the Everlasting Hills*, a book detailing the life of Jesus and his impact on history.

We often spoke about religion and spirituality. Max told me he admired my faith, even envied it. But he couldn't get there himself. While he chose not to practice a formal religion, his code of conduct and virtues were consistent with those of the many people I know who do. Max pursued the path he felt comfortable with—the intellectual and academic investigation of religion and spirituality.

So in the prime of his life, Max was consumed by cancer just twelve days before our fourth wedding anniversary. Only six months had passed from the time of diagnosis to his death.

Our dear friend Dr. Viva Ettin described a conversation she had with Max during his chemotherapy. Still embracing what life had to offer him, he said to her, "I have wines that I have laid down for twenty years that I will not drink. I have no desire to drink or eat, but the other day I had a glass of water. It tasted so fresh and crisp and sparkling. What pleasure it gave me. The other day I sat with Janis at the kitchen table looking at the sunlight with her. What pleasure."

Viva shared what Max told her on the day he found out that his cancer had metastasized to his lungs and that his time on earth was short. She asked him what he wanted to do with his last months. He said, "I want to spend every last moment with Janis and Tanner."

Then he cried.

In the week before he died, we talked in a way we never had before. He didn't rail against his disease or his impending death. Max said, "It's our love and my deep belief in our marriage and family that have carried me through these difficult months." Near the end he told me, "It's only our love that gives me the courage to face death. It's easier for me because I'm leaving. It will be harder for you because you are being left behind."

But one of the most startling comments he made during that last week was, "You will find someone else, and you will remarry. And it will be even better than what we have had."

I replied, "That's impossible." There's no way I believed I'd ever find this kind of love again.

"No, it's not," he said, "because I will be there. My love will never die. It's immutable."

That's what I put on his gravestone in the Yountville cemetery where he asked to be buried.

Max Besler
1948–2004
Our Immutable Love
Janis and Tanner

In his final two months, Max spent a great deal of time during the day with our friend and housekeeper, Helen. Max insisted that I continue working, so I established a routine of going to the office daily and, when possible on certain days, I'd drive home for a visit. I think he just didn't want me to see what he was going through. Thankfully Helen was with Max when I couldn't be. Helen, a believer in God, told me that her conversations with Max, the skeptic, were telling. She said she and Max were sitting at the kitchen table one day with the sun shining when it suddenly began to pour down rain. "We both just stopped and looked," Helen recalled. "I told him, 'I know you have questions about God, but this is something God created for us today.'"

"After you're gone," Helen told Max, "if you can find a way, let us know that there's something out there, that it just doesn't end."

He agreed he would find a way to let us both know, Helen said. "But it will be up to you two to see it," he told her.

A day or so before he died, Max said to me, "I need a box. The directions are in a box. I need directions to the place I'm going. Can you come along? Oh, I forgot, you cannot."

As much as that comment stung with the pain of our impending separation, I think he was actively seeking a path to the other side. And his comment to Helen foreshadowed events to come.

"It will be up to you two to see it."

CHAPTER 4

The Valley of the Shadow of Death

Max died at 12:44 p.m. on Saturday, May 8, 2004. As he took his last breath, seven of us, his friends and family, gathered around him. We were in the living room of our home in Sacramento. Max, now shrunken to a bony 138 pounds from his muscular 205-pound frame, was lying peacefully on the narrow hospital bed brought in by hospice several days earlier. Tanner and I had positioned the bed in the middle of the room next to our fireplace so he would be front and center, surrounded by those who loved him.

I wanted Max to be in his home, not the hospital, when he died. And I wanted very much for his family and friends to usher him out so he would not be alone in his final hours. As I watched him sleeping under the heavy influence of morphine, I was so sad I felt as if I could howl in agony. Yet I contained my sorrow to protect my son. Somehow I found the courage to behave reasonably, even though I knew I was perilously close to coming unhinged.

We had reached the point where we knew Max's death was imminent and would be a blessing for him. He had suffered enough. I found myself holding my breath as we waited for him to take his last breath. Time stood still. I was slumped over in a chair next to Max on his right, and Tanner was situated to his left. I held Max's thin, lifeless hand on one side and stretched over the bed to clutch Tanner's plump, warm hand in my other one. Tanner did the same, creating a seamless link among the three of us. Nothing in my life had prepared me for this. I hadn't read any books on how to help people die. I'd never asked anyone for advice on how to cope with this enormous and important life moment. And yet, here it was. Max was dying, and he would soon be gone. Forever. I was going to live the rest of my life without him. And the family that Tanner, Max, and I had created would no longer exist. How was I supposed to continue?

I had set aside my Bible on an end table earlier that morning. Catching it out of the corner of my eye, I quietly reached over and lifted it from the table, opening it to the marker I had left at Psalm 23. Asking the others to join hands with Tanner and me, I recited the words. "The Lord is my shepherd; I shall not want..."

In the backyard beneath the overhang of the roof just outside the door were two heavy wind chimes that Max and I had hung several years before. Both were sizable. One, made of wood with suspended shiny metal tubes, produced a deep musical sound when it rang, while the other one, shaped in a triangle, reminded me of the gong of a buoy at sea. I thought it was fitting that they both rang the instant Max died, filling the house with rich, melodious tones. As a group we stopped to listen. Someone said the ringing recalled the music of a pipe organ playing in a cathedral. As we turned our heads in unison to watch the chimes perform, we noticed something very peculiar. There was no wind.

Reflecting on that moment, I am still struck by how fragile and thin the veil is between being alive and being dead. One breath, one still moment, then silence, and the person you know and love slips away, never to be felt again.

Death presents a paradox for those of us left behind. If we believe in heaven or an afterlife or a survival of consciousness in some form, why do we suffer such great pain with the death of a loved one? I think it's because even with all the power of love, it's the ongoing physical and mental interaction that expresses that love. So as we lose that interaction, how do we deal with the grief? I learned an important lesson from a dear friend, the Reverend Jesse Vaughan.

A true man of God, Jesse is an Episcopalian minister who recently retired as headmaster of St. Michael's Episcopal Day School in Sacramento. I met him while serving on a local board. When Max was diagnosed, Jesse was one of the first visitors to our house. Somehow he knew to come right away, and I'll always remember his face at the front door. I have found that while you forget much in life, you never forget who was there for you during challenging times. I will always be grateful for that visit from Jesse.

Months later I asked him, "How do you deal with it—the finality of the loss? How do you ever get used to it?"

He answered quietly, as is his way. "It's their essence that you never forget. It lives on inside you." I was comforted by Jesse's observation and often thought of it in my toughest hours.

Our friends left in the early afternoon, taking Tanner with them, and the funeral home came to take Max's body. I made my way to the master bedroom to change my clothes before going to a friend's home to rest. That's when I saw that the light above the sink in the master bathroom was out. I noticed because it had never gone out before. Tanner and I had lived there since 1998 and never replaced that bulb. Now, the day Max died, it was out. This struck me as odd, but then again, lights do burn out. Regardless, I didn't have the energy or mental acuity in those early moments after Max's passing to think meaningfully about anything. I could barely put one foot in front of the other.

We held Max's funeral at Trinity Cathedral Church in downtown Sacramento. Jesse conducted the service, and several hundred people filled the church to honor Max, who was well loved and respected in the Sacramento community. The service began with the pallbearers carrying his coffin down the aisle to the front of the sanctuary. Tanner was a pallbearer, so he was in front of me. I was to follow with my brother and sister-in-law, Kurt and Marky Olson, accompanying me on each side. But just as we were to head down the aisle, I froze. I turned to Marky and said, "I don't think I can do this."

At that moment something highly unlikely occurred. An open door to an anteroom off the front of the church slowly closed with a loud slam. This was not a delicate door. It was substantial. No one was near it, and, again, there was no wind. It closed without anyone touching it, which seemed impossible. It startled all three of us. After a few seconds, Marky said, "I think Max wants you to do it, and I know you can." She was right. As we walked arm in arm down the long center aisle to the front of the sanctuary, I felt urged to take each step. I also felt enveloped by the love and generous outpouring of support from those in the congregation. Family and friends from Max's world, Tanner's world, and mine were there. The warmth of their presence filled my empty heart and gave me courage.

It wasn't until I had time to reflect later in the week that I thought about the events that were now forming a pattern. Weighty chimes play in perfectly still air. A lightbulb that just happens to go out on the day of Max's death. Then a door too heavy to close on its own closes on its own. What—if anything— was going on? Maybe I was confused, under a blanket of grief. Maybe I'd imagined all of it. Or maybe it was nothing—just coincidence.

I made up my mind to focus on Tanner and spend time with friends and family. These were the hardest days of my life, and I was ill prepared. I had never lost anyone to death before, and each day, I felt like I was falling into quicksand. I needed the security and comfort of my loved ones; I was barely functioning. Thinking about the odd occurrences would have to wait.

For now I was consumed by my grief, absorbing an entirely new life experience. And I was beginning to realize that once the rituals of saying good-bye are over, sympathy from others gradually begins to wane. But grief doesn't. It's the most private emotion I've ever known. Anyone who has mourned a loved one understands the pain. It feels simply unbearable, and you keep asking yourself if you can go on. Somehow you do.

CHAPTER 5

Strange Events Unfold

A week after Max's death, I took Casey, our yellow Lab, for a long walk along the American River pathway to get some exercise and clear my mind. It was Saturday morning, around seven a.m., and Tanner was asleep in his room. I returned about an hour later, and as I was unhooking Casey's leash from his collar, I glanced up at the large, round Ethan Allen clock over our fireplace in the living room, where Max had died. That's when I saw something odd. The clock had stopped—at 12:44, the exact time of Max's death. At first I didn't process it. I thought, *Time to get Tanner up for breakfast.* Then it sank in. How could the clock show the time of Max's death instead of eight o'clock, the proper time? I turned around and walked to Tanner's bedroom to wake him, half hoping that when we returned, the clock would show the correct time.

"Wake up. Wake up. You're not going to believe what I just saw," I told Tanner. Like a normal fourteen-year-old, Tanner pulled back the covers and stumbled sleepily down the hallway behind me to the living room.

The day Max died, those of us who were with him had noted the time of 12:44. I had also written the time of death in a small black notebook to share with the appropriate authorities. It was not a guess or an approximation. It was an exact time. Tanner knew it as well as I did.

"Look, Tanner," I said, pointing at the big clock. He glanced up. His eyes became big and round, and he opened his mouth as if to say something, but no words came out. Instead he just kept staring until finally he turned back to look at me.

He muttered two words: "No way."

Together we stared at the clock while Casey fussed at our feet. There didn't seem to be any explanation. The night before, when I went to bed after Tanner was already asleep, the clock was running fine. No one else was in the house. Besides, the clock was too heavy and positioned too awkwardly for someone to lift it over the fireplace mantel to change the time. Neither Tanner nor I could manage it.

"I don't understand how this could happen," I said. I was curious more than anything else. Was this part of a sequence of connected events, or was it just another isolated coincidence? Did it mean anything? The chimes playing without wind and the lightbulb blowing out on the day Max died, the church door closing by itself—and now this.

"Mom, maybe it needs a new battery. We can't change it, but we can get some help to pull it down," Tanner offered, thankfully interrupting my thoughts. "And it's probably just a coincidence that it stopped at 12:44."

"Yes, that's probably it," I said, uncertain deep down that it was that simple but unwilling to consider the idea that it might be more. I wanted a neat, pat answer. There was too much on my plate. The shock of Max's diagnosis, his agonizing battle with cancer, and his heartbreaking death six months later had taken a toll on me. He had died only seven days ago. I was barely functioning.

"I think I'll go back to bed," Tanner said. Whatever this mystery was with the clock and whatever grief I was feeling, it was Tanner who grounded me in what was essential. I needed to stay strong and rational for him.

The clock stayed at 12:44 until Wednesday, when Helen came. When I arrived home in the evening I found a note from her. It said the lights had flickered and the clock had restarted simultaneously. She had not touched the clock or replaced the battery.

"I think Max may have paid us a visit," Helen wrote in her note.

About two weeks later, I was sitting on the couch in our living room with Casey at my feet. I was watching a *Law & Order* rerun and writing thank-you notes to the many people who had sent condolences after Max's death. Tanner was with his dad at his home. Suddenly I heard what initially sounded like a clanging noise coming from the guest bedroom area, where Max had spent his last month. *What on earth is that?* I wondered. I picked up the remote and turned down the TV so I could listen more carefully. Casey didn't appear to hear it, which was curious.

I rose from the couch and walked directly toward the sound. It was coming from the bathroom in the guest suite. As I got closer, the noise sounded like someone was hammering a nail into the wall. I entered the bathroom and froze. To the left of the mirror and about two feet above the commode, the wall was pulsating. That's right. It was literally pulsating. Instead of a normal flat wall, what I saw was a wall that was moving in a wavelike motion. Equally confounding, the waves didn't appear to be in sync with the noise, which had a staccato beat. The movement in the wall was more like a smooth, legato wave, rising and receding softly under the plaster. I stood motionless, telling myself that even though I knew what I saw and heard, the idea of it actually occurring was absurd. *This can't be happening*, I said to myself.

Okay, I thought, *time to find the practical, no-nonsense answer to this mystery*—in other words, the "real" reason. I hadn't started the washing machine, which was directly behind the bathroom wall. Yet it sounded as if it might be hitting against the wall, so I checked the laundry room. Maybe it was on some delayed setting. Nothing. All right, perhaps it was raining or the wind was blowing. Maybe a power line got loose and was banging against the roof. I quickly ran out the front door. No rain. No storm. No wind. No downed lines. Nothing. I darted back inside and returned swiftly to the bathroom. It was over.

The noise and pulsating had lasted only about five minutes, I think. It was so weird that I thought I must have imagined it. I was way too tired, too worn-out. I needed to get a grip. But there was a tiny voice in the corner of my mind telling me I knew I hadn't manufactured it because I wouldn't know where to begin to do so. My strong desire to find an ordinary answer that would substantiate normalcy was doing battle with the sneaking suspicion that something highly extraordinary was happening. I made the decision to go with ordinary. I would call a plumber and a pest control company. They would have an answer.

The plumber arrived two days later to inspect the pipes in the wall above the commode next to the mirror. I didn't tell him anything but just asked if the pipes could cause noises or vibrations in the wall. He checked the plumbing and said it rose only to the height of the toilet, so that couldn't have been the problem. The pest control company came out next. I wanted to see whether a rodent or other animal could have been the source by wriggling down behind the wallboard somehow. The workers climbed around in the attic, shining their flashlights everywhere for evidence of rodents, but found nothing.

I had a real conundrum on my hands. But stronger than this quandary was my will to bring as much order to my life as possible. I suppressed not only this unexplained phenomenon but the other events as well. I told myself it was not only irrational thinking; it was counterproductive to my health, to raising Tanner, and to my work. I would live with the mystery because it was the only way to survive my grief.

On Father's Day 2004, a little more than a month after Max died, the grief was still raw, and I was feeling particularly melancholy. I kept thinking about how much Max and Tanner loved each other. Max wasn't Tanner's biological father and could never replace his own dad, but Max was like a father in every other way. Their positive chemistry was palpable from the beginning, and Max taught Tanner a great deal about history, politics, and culture. They naturally gravitated to each other, and the love between them was obvious.

On that Sunday, I was once again sitting on the couch in our living room, this time rocking back and forth, listening to Celine Dion's song "Because You Loved Me," which we had played at Max's funeral. I was reliving the service and wallowing in my sorrow. Without warning, I began to feel agitated, as if I should be doing something, should move off the couch. I wandered into the library, where Max spent a great deal of time reading and listening to his classical music. He loved this room more than any of the others in our home. It was an inviting room with high vaulted ceilings and floor-to-ceiling built-in bookshelves on every wall, all of them crammed with books. The only space without books was the bay window facing our front yard. I never counted the books, most of which were Max's, but there must have been at least a thousand.

As I circled the library a few times, I eventually stopped and randomly pulled a book off a shelf. I was thumbing through it when a card fell out and landed on the floor. The card's envelope was addressed to Max in what looked to be a woman's handwriting. I am ashamed to say that my first thought was, *Oh no, please don't let me find out that Max was having an affair.* I hurriedly opened the card and discovered it was from his mother, Margaret Besler, who had given it to Max for Father's Day the previous year. She had written, "I've never seen you this happy in your life. It's because you have a family."

I couldn't believe my eyes. How did this card end up in my hands on Father's Day one year later? How did I choose that book from the thousands on the shelves? What were the odds? Who or what was trying to comfort me? How could I possibly arrive at this book on this holiday and discover a message that would provide such needed solace?

Throughout the summer when I was home, I would leave the front screen door closed but would open the heavy front door to cool the house. Several times I clearly heard a loud knock on the door, only to find no one there. And sometimes when I forgot to latch the screen door it would open and shut on its own. While I found it odd, I dismissed it. However, a kernel was beginning to germinate. I began keeping a private list of the strange occurrences. I couldn't resist. I was having an increasingly difficult time ignoring these phenomena. What did they mean, if anything? Should I be doing something with all this?

It took a long time to deal with Max's possessions. I felt disloyal, as if I were abandoning Max, when I let go of the material items he wore, valued, or held. There are all the practical items, such as suits, slacks, shirts, and jackets. Then there are the more personal items: his trumpet from high school, his treasured record albums from the 1960s, his dad's medals from World War II, his massive assemblage of classical CDs, his beloved books. But of all his possessions, it was his shoes that spoke to me. Something about them prevented me from touching them. I think it's because he loved his shoes and took such care of them. He'd keep them well shined and arranged in his closet by color. They were a "collection" to Max. And when he put them on, he stood proud. I'd often stare at them in the closet thinking I should give them to someone who could use them, and then when I reached down to gather a pair, I would become immobile. I couldn't touch them, let alone bring myself to move them out of the house. But after a while, I realized I had to do it. So on a Saturday night I pulled together his clothes and shoes to give them to Goodwill, keeping a few of his favorite ties and shirts for Tanner and a sweater Marky had asked for. Separately, I packed one small box to keep, a very special box for the intimate items I could never part with: his round tortoiseshell glasses, his worn black wallet with every school picture of Tanner from fifth to eighth grade, his American flag from his service in the air force, a tiny burgundy hairbrush that he used every morning after he showered, and some favorite photos. The next day I packed most of his books too, knowing the public library would make good use of them. That night the lights flickered prominently in the kitchen.

I dealt with my grief by focusing on Tanner and my work. I had plenty to keep me busy. Sacramento is not one of the largest cities in the country, but it's the capital of California, which has the eighth-largest economy in the world. So we had much to deal with at the newspaper.

In early 2005, we held an offsite retreat in Yountville, California, for *The Bee's* management team. The team stayed at a local hotel, and I stayed in our Yountville home. I had been there only once since Max had died, and though I had donated some of Max's books at our Sacramento home, the Yountville home still had all his books on the shelves. It looked much the same as it had when he was last there.

I've always been a dedicated walker, so I took off for an hour-long walk before the morning meeting. I left at about six a.m. and followed my favorite route, about three miles long. When I returned, I went to the kitchen for some coffee. I was surprised to see the digital clock on the stove showing 12:44. Interestingly, the digital clock on the microwave, which was next to the stove, correctly said 7:15, making a power outage seem like an unlikely explanation. And now I knew that these strange phenomena were not exclusive to our Sacramento home.

Shortly afterward, back in Sacramento, I experienced something that seemed to go a step further and in a new direction. Unlike clocks stopping, lights flickering, a plumbing challenge, or an errant screen door, this was provocative in an entirely different way. I came home from work one evening and decided to soak in the bathtub of our master bath. I was relaxing in the tub, wearing my chunky glasses because I was reading a book, when I noticed something I had never seen before. Beautiful golden threads were floating about a foot from my eyes. At first

I thought it had to be my imagination or even a hallucination. I blinked. I stared. Slowly I became captivated by their elegance and grace.

Here were a handful of magnificent silky golden threads sailing horizontally in front of my face. Each was about nine or ten inches long. They looked similar to the corn silk found on corn on the cob. The threads weren't connected to the wall, to one another, or to anything else. They were afloat in space, and they were glistening. I was mesmerized by their exquisite and delicate gracefulness. The whole experience felt poetic, as if I were being transported to an ethereal place. It reminded me of the times in nature when I've seen a perfect rainbow arching over mountains or snow twinkling on treetops with just the right contours of light. I had no idea what prompted these threads, but I took luxurious pleasure in them.

Coming back to reality after a few minutes, I took off my glasses to see if they were smudged and had merely created an illusion. I placed them on the rim of the tub and looked straight out in front of me again. And there they were. I could still see the luminous threads. I rubbed my eyes. I opened them again. The enchanted threads remained. I slowly reached out to touch one. It dissipated under the weight of my finger. I sat still and stared at them, lost in the moment so deeply that I wasn't even questioning what in heaven's name was going on.

Books continued to remind me of Max at crucial times. Several months after the golden threads appeared, I returned to Yountville for the weekend. One of our favorite places for dinner had been Bistro Jeanty, where Max and I would sit next to each other at the bar. On this visit, I walked to the restaurant and sat at our favorite spot at the bar, with a novel to pass the time and to minimize the insecurity I felt about eating out alone. After dinner I walked home and continued to read in the small library, Max's favorite room in our Napa home, just as it was in our Sacramento home. I glanced up and caught sight of a book with a plain black-and-white cover. For some reason, I felt compelled to stand up and pull down the book, just as I had done in Sacramento when I found the comforting Father's Day card from Max's mother. Once again, something fell out. It was a small piece of paper, and as I bent down to retrieve it, I could see it was a credit card receipt.

Looking closer, I read it and froze. It was a receipt for a dinner that Max and I had enjoyed at Bistro Jeanty two years earlier. Not just on any date, but two years earlier to the day. Maybe a restaurant receipt falling from a book is not unusual. And we did visit Bistro Jeanty frequently. But from the same date exactly, in a randomly chosen book among hundreds, on a night when I had just been at the same restaurant? That seemed highly improbable.

About a month later, I was reading in the same library when my eye again caught a specific book on the shelf. I don't know why I chose it from an entire wall of books. I pulled it down and saw that it focused on the writings of Marcus Aurelius, the Roman emperor whose most famous work is *Meditations*. Several pages were dog-eared.

I opened to the first marked page. Two quotes had been underlined. The first was "Despise not death, but welcome it, for nature wills it like all else."

The second was "Constantly regard the universe as one living being, having one substance and one soul; and observe how all things have reference to one perception.... Observe too the continuous spinning of the thread and the contexture of the web."

I was overcome. Was Max reading this just prior to his death? We made frequent trips to Yountville in his last months before he became unable to travel. Was he seeking to understand his plight? Or was I experiencing this independently of him? More intriguing, did this have some connection or reference to the threads I saw in the bathtub? Were they symbolic of this "spinning of the thread and the contexture of the web"? Why had I selected this book from the hundreds on the shelves? Was I supposed to be getting a message?

CHAPTER 6

The Journey Begins

As the coincidences and mysterious occurrences piled up in the first year after Max's death, I remained in denial. I observed or experienced whatever was occurring, but I suppressed it with my usual rationale of focusing on the priorities of everyday life. I resisted talking to others about it primarily because I was embarrassed. I was worried they would judge me, thinking I had simply gone off my rocker.

But the hand on the mirror in May 2005 on the first anniversary of Max's death changed everything. It unmoored me in ways none of the previous events had. Not only was I absolutely certain I hadn't imagined it, because Tanner witnessed the handprint with me, but the stunning nature of the powdery print was too shocking to ignore. It necessitated a response. I couldn't rationalize it away as I had the stopped time on the clock or the sounds in the wall, believing that these had practical explanations that I just couldn't confirm.

The handprint forced me to confront the truth instead of

suppressing it. I was going to have to quit being so circumspect and find someone I could confide in and get some feedback from. The most logical person was Helen, since she had witnessed some of the events and had spoken to Max before he died about his hoping to reconnect with us from the other side. I did speak to her cautiously, but I didn't want to appear vulnerable with her since she was working for me. And it didn't seem fair to burden her, although she certainly had an open mind. Of course there was Tanner. He had witnessed the chimes ringing with no wind, the clock stopping at 12:44, and, more significantly, the handprint. But my maternal instinct to protect him overrode everything else. I didn't want to distract him from his schoolwork or give him a reason to worry. After all, he was only fifteen years old.

Ultimately I decided to talk with my sister, Signe Feldman, and my sister-in-law, Marky, both of whom I love and trust and am extremely close to. Signe lives in Dallas, and Marky lives in Seattle, so our conversations were over the phone. They were always patient and understanding. But I think I only managed to worry them. They probably thought that whatever I was experiencing was associated with my grief.

I also reached out to a few of my closest friends who could be trusted to keep our discussions confidential. They were sympathetic listeners, but, again, I think I just increased their concern for me. Sure, they were kind, polite, and supportive. But to be fair, they must have also thought I was a bit wacko. It had to have been pretty weird to absorb, and it's not surprising they would attribute my experiences of these phenomena to my grief.

About that time something fortuitous happened. Max, Tanner, and I had been planning a trip to Italy before Max was diagnosed in the fall of 2003. Max had been very excited because he was knowledgeable about Italy's famous painters, sculptors, poets, and musicians and was a huge fan of the museums and art collections. He had hoped to visit the ancient ruins since he was intrigued by architecture as well. But more than anything else, he loved Italy's wine and food.

I had an idea I thought might be helpful. I told Tanner we would take the trip in Max's honor. We agreed Max would be happy knowing we were going to celebrate his life. I thought of it not only as precious time with Tanner, reflecting together, but also as time to consider what had been going on since Max died. The trip would allow me to get away from the distractions and time constraints of daily life and clear my mind. Maybe I would find some answers. Or at least I would begin to ask better questions.

Our dear friends Carolyn and Mike Valenti and their son, Bryan, who was a good buddy of Tanner's, were also planning a trip to Italy, so we decided to meet them there. We toured Rome and Florence together, and I did my best to relax and go with the flow. But there were also painful moments when I thought about Max and craved his presence. Grief comes in waves, and just when you think you're fine, you're not. But at least I was making some progress.

As we toured the Uffizi, climbed the steps of the Colosseum, roamed the Pantheon, and quietly walked through St. Peter's Basilica, I slowly felt myself unwinding. I was still unsure about what the handprint and the other phenomena meant. I couldn't explain them to myself, let alone anyone else. But I was beginning to acknowledge that these events were valid. Instead of denying and suppressing what had happened, I could feel myself opening up. Curiosity was replacing fear. I wanted to know what was going on.

THE HAND ON THE MIRROR

After a week in Rome and Florence, we said good-bye to our friends, and Tanner and I headed to the Italian Riviera on our own. One day, just before sunset, we were strolling through the beautiful village of Portofino, admiring the pastel houses lining the harbor and talking about the eclectic array of boats, with magnificent yachts anchored next to humble fishing boats. The afternoon sun was casting a magical glow on the turquoise water, and I knew it was an enchanted moment. But I never dreamed how astounding it would turn out to be.

I had purchased a disposable Kodak camera (no camera phones in 2005) when we arrived in Italy because I had somehow managed to jam my point-and-shoot camera on the plane and it wasn't operating properly. I pulled out the disposable camera and suggested to Tanner that we stop and ask someone to take our picture. In no time at all, a friendly passerby helped us record the moment as we stood at the water's edge. When we arrived back in Sacramento, I had the photos developed and picked them up a few days later. I thumbed through all the photos until I found the one with Tanner and me standing at the edge of the harbor. The passerby had taken a very lovely photo for us.

On closer examination, I noticed something astonishing. Behind us in the photo was the stern of a modest fishing boat floating at anchor in the harbor about thirty yards away. The name of the boat, painted on the stern, was lined up perfectly between my shoulder and Tanner's, just where Max would have stood had he made the trip and been in the photo. I squinted to read the name of the boat and saw three simple letters: MAX.

This was impossible. I stared at the photo. Was this yet another extraordinary coincidence? The odds of this occurring seemed astronomical—that only these three letters on the boat would appear, that they would be placed so perfectly between us, that they would spell out Max's name, that a complete stranger would snap this particular angle in such a quick fashion without knowing our story.

I knew at that moment that the journey I had begun in Italy needed to continue back home. I just didn't know how to get started. Talking a little more openly now to a close confidant, I shared the idea that I wanted to learn more about the spiritual realm. This friend suggested something quite obvious. Why not do what I had observed in more than thirty years in the newspaper business—research and investigate? It was an epiphany and served as the pivotal launching point for what would become a transformational journey of spiritual growth and understanding. I realized that I needed to quit reacting as a bystander. I decided to learn as much as I could about these incidents (I didn't even know what to call them) by reading and talking with experts. My journey would span eight years and eventually take me across the country to interview scientists, professors, physicists, and spiritual practitioners. But for now I was just starting—tentatively.

My first stop was to research New Age literature at East West Books not far from my home in Sacramento. I decided to go in disguise. Although the Sacramento region is comprised of seven counties and a population of nearly 2.5 million, it is a small community in many ways. As publisher of the local newspaper, I was relatively recognizable. It didn't seem like a good idea to be seen in this setting, whether by the general public or by The Bee's employees. After all, the abstract and mysterious metaphysical world is miles apart from the fact-based and analytical newspaper world. I felt I had an obligation to protect the paper's image. So I wore a nondescript baseball cap pulled down low over my eyes, which were hidden behind huge dark sunglasses. And I chose baggy gray sweatpants and a sweatshirt to complement the whole effect. In short, I looked ridiculous. I made no eye contact with anyone as I roamed aimlessly around the aisles pretending to know exactly what I was doing but having absolutely no clue what that was.

Fortunately, the store had helpful signs to tell me what category was offered on each bookshelf, just as regular bookstores do, so I decided to zero in accordingly. Loads of books addressed astrology, spirituality, the metaphysical, health and wellness, yoga, meditation, religion, and psychology, to name just a few. I recognized some of the books and authors, such as Eckhart Tolle, Deepak Chopra, Caroline Myss, James Redfield, Paulo Coelho, Miguel Ruiz, and Brian Weiss. But overall I was just wandering around. I started wondering what I was even doing there when I began to notice soothing New Age music in the background creating an ambience that reminded me of the music played at the spa when I get a massage. I assumed they were playing an Enya or Yanni CD. So I relaxed a bit.

Gathering my courage, I selected a few books and slid up to the counter. While I was waiting in line, trying to be invisible, I noticed that most of the people in the store were women. And interestingly, they had a similar style to one another. It was very natural. Lots of long beautiful hair and no makeup, which I envied because they could get away with it, and they were wearing Birkenstock sandals. I own a pair of Birkenstock sandals myself, so I recognized them immediately. And what was I wearing on my feet? Tennis shoes. Big, fat, heavy tennis shoes. My "disguise" made me stand out like a traffic light.

Safely at home and out of my "disguise," I read my newly

purchased books. Over the next month, they whetted my appetite for more.

Then I remembered Robin. In 1998, shortly after I started at *The Bee*, I called on a consultant who worked with major newspapers to help us develop a growth strategy that would serve the readers and the company. The consultant brought his knowledge and expertise to us as we worked up our plans. But the most interesting thing about him was his unusual blend of business sophistication and strong interest in the human dimension of corporate life. As we were completing the engagement, he suggested I contact Dr. Robin Van Doren, who was living in Sacramento. He told me I would find her very enlightening on a personal level.

I followed up and met with Robin for the first time in 1998, not really knowing what to expect. She lived near downtown Sacramento in a charming California-style bungalow beautifully appointed with treasures and art from her worldwide travels. I felt immediately comfortable with her. Robin's eyes sparkled, and her broad smile seemed to emit sunshine. She greeted me and extended a firm handshake. *This sixty-something woman knows herself and is comfortable with who she is*, I thought.

As I sat on her couch, I began to wonder why I was even there. I liked her, but my life was running smoothly at that point. We chatted a bit, mainly small talk, and eventually I said, "Well, I'm not sure what I'm doing here, so I guess I'll leave now." I felt silly.

Without hesitation she replied, "No problem. You'll know when you're ready, and you'll come back then."

I enjoyed meeting her, but I left doubting we would ever get together again. Life was good, and I didn't have any reason to be there.

This time, things were different. Max had died, and my life had been turned upside down. Strange things were happening. I needed guidance. But how do you describe these events to someone you barely know and still maintain a modicum of credibility? With a great deal of hesitation, I called Robin. We had not spoken in seven years, but something deep inside told me I would be safe with her and she would advise me without judgment or skepticism. As important, she had a reputation as a trustworthy confidant. I met with her a number of times and consulted with her on the phone.

For the last thirty-five years Robin has conducted seminars and facilitated groups to support trust in inner wisdom and the practice of seeing the beloved in all beings. A basic assumption of this work is that existence has multiple layers.

An exceptional woman with extraordinary talents and experiences, Robin remembers as a small child communicating with her grandmother after she passed away. Robin's mother found this disturbing and quickly discouraged it. But later, while completing her bachelor's degree at Radcliffe, Robin had another experience that convinced her that there is more going on than most people think. She was taking an oral exam from a professor and was questioned on a subject she knew very little about. Her responses and performance were later described as brilliant. The only explanation, she determined, was that she must have been reading the professor's mind or using mental telepathy. As she jokes about it today, "If you read someone's mind, they think you're brilliant."

After Radcliffe, Robin married and had children. She moved to New York and taught school in Harlem. Her interest in education led her to study the brain. She attended meetings of the Orton Society (now the International Dyslexia Association) and continued working with children to study how they learn. Robin was accepted at Columbia University in the doctorate program in education. She was later asked to leave because, as her adviser, who was the head of the department, put it, "One of us has to go."

This difference of opinion started at a seminar where Robin was presenting. She gave everyone pieces of paper and asked them to make a sculpture from them. It was, she says, an exercise in the exploration of freedom. Columbia's response was— yes, great, but not here. She came away feeling that academia disapproved of experiential learning. "People teach as they were taught, so nothing moves," Robin said.

Seeing no way to reconcile with Columbia, she transferred to Fairleigh Dickinson University, where she completed her doctorate in education and began lecturing on the neurological basis for learning. Her mother ran a center at the New School of New York, where Robin met the noted lecturer, author, and scholar Jean Houston, the founder of the Human Potential Movement, which explores the unlimited possibilities of the mind. Houston worked on the mechanics of greatness with psychoanalyst Carl Jung, inventor Buckminster Fuller, author Aldous Huxley, and a number of U.S. astronauts. Robin and Jean began a long friendship and a ten-year partnership conducting lectures and seminars together.

Robin lived in New York until she was forty. One rainy night, a taxi hit her while she was crossing the street. She remembers the classic characteristics of a near-death experience, leaving her body and floating above, watching the event unfold. She says she saw God, though she had never gone to church in her life. For the next six months she lived in what she describes as "a sea of love." People came from all over the country to help her because she couldn't move. She eventually recovered, and her strong belief today is that God is knowable and unknowable and is the source of all there is.

In her early forties, during her postdoctoral fellowship at the University of Alabama, Robin was an assistant to Joseph Campbell, the noted mythologist and author of *The Power of Myth* and *The Hero with a Thousand Faces*, at a seminar in Southern California. She fell in love with the city of Ojai. There she started a spiritual and educational center called Hamsayeh, which in Persian means "shared shade of the wall."

Robin decided to experience places where the things we call magic happen with hardly an eyebrow raised. She moved to India and Indonesia for five years. She says she learned a great deal but realized she would always be a guest, and guests are not supposed to change things. So she moved back to California, this time to Sacramento.

Robin's spiritual experiences and knowledge fell far outside mine. Not only was my understanding of the afterlife limited to my Presbyterian upbringing, but I worked in an industry that was a breeding ground for skepticism about almost anything. The business of publishing required a mainstream professional demeanor and lifestyle (witness my disguise in the New Age bookstore). Journalists can be eccentric; the business side of newspaper management isn't.

But I had certainly learned about more esoteric spiritual views over four decades of adult life, especially living in California. And thanks to my education-minded parents and my career, I felt that curiosity, new concepts, and personal growth added value to work and life. I was open to hearing what Robin had to say.

She has taught me that the boundary between life and

death is more porous than we've been led to believe. When we talk about another dimension, she believes it's actually here; you just can't see it. She says, "You can talk about the brain as much as you like, but it's like talking about a radio. It's just a receiving station—it doesn't do original programming."

A teacher once told her that if someone gives you a stone, that stone has energy. Don't take it if you don't want the energy. All things have energy. What is energy? It's everything. When it's concentrated, form occurs.

Robin confirmed my feeling that I didn't need to fear the events that followed Max's death. She believed that what I saw was some aspect of Max. She believed that some part of him got stuck or was lost, not able to find the path.

Robin described the insights that come to her as "more like a sense of being enormously helped." Her insights come through her body—sort of a tingle. She feels guided but not by a guide. It's a knowing. Boundaries between levels become transparent. The last time I visited Robin she reminded me that as we grow up we all acquire filters that hamper or preclude our ability to listen to the spirit world that coexists with us. Her parting advice was, "Pay attention."

I was new at this and incredibly fortunate to have met someone of Robin's caliber as my first exposure to a spiritual practitioner. Not only was she highly educated and knowledgeable; she was honest and well intentioned. I trusted and respected her immediately. And she never disappointed me.

But as with most things in life, not everyone practicing in a field is on the up-and-up. Anyone can profess to possess powers and capabilities. It doesn't mean they do. And people can pretend to be well intentioned. It doesn't mean they are. In the very beginning of my journey, I was naïve to think I wouldn't end up meeting a few quacks. In fact, I did. Fortunately, they were, indeed, only a few.

One example is a session I had with an "energy healer" in San Francisco. I had heard about this individual from a "friend of a friend" and called to schedule an appointment with him. I explained that I wanted to talk to him about his work and possibly have a session as well, depending on what transpired. I had no intention of discussing my personal experiences. I was strictly seeking to educate myself and discover what offerings existed out there in this curious new world I was investigating. As with the New Age bookstore, I felt intimidated by my lack of exposure.

Our meeting was scheduled for a Saturday morning, and it wasn't easy finding his office. I was driving over from Sacramento, and it was raining hard. Of course I got lost (a common affliction for me), so I was about ten minutes late. Knocking loudly on the door of what appeared to be a triplex, I soon found myself facing an enormous man in the doorway. He was dressed from head to toe in brown: brown shirt, brown pants, brown moccasins. His outfit looked like those scrub suits you see in hospitals, more like pajamas than street clothes. Only instead of green, the color was, yes, brown. He smiled a toothy smile from under a somewhat scraggly beard and opened the door wide, inviting me in. We introduced ourselves, and he led me down a short hall to a separate room. I noticed there was no one else around in the hallway, but I assumed that was because it was a Saturday.

As we entered the small room, I was immediately struck by a whiff of the musky aroma of incense. On a small wicker table was a glowing ember in a glass bowl, easy to see because the room was so dark. The shades over the window were pulled shut, and there was only one small lamp situated next to the incense on the table. It looked like a fake Tiffany. Two diminutive armchairs flanked the table. The only other furniture was a massage table in the middle of the room. We seated ourselves in the chairs, and the "healer" began describing his abilities to me.

"I am able to invoke a power that is intangible," he said. "Think of it as a life force." He explained that he was a conduit for bringing healing energy forward and channeling it to me. As he was speaking, I noticed I was beginning to sweat, and it wasn't because I was hot. I was getting an uneasy feeling in my gut.

"I can restore balance and harmony to the energy system in your body by tracing my hand over your skin along certain energy pathways," he explained. He warned me that if one of my chakras was blocked, it could affect my organs, so we would start with him checking my chakras.

He stood and said I needed to climb up onto the massage table for our session to begin. I had worn a pair of leggings and a long-sleeved T-shirt that day, thinking I might need to lie down on a massage table if we had a full session. I stood up from my chair to walk to the table when I heard him say, "Well, you have to take your clothes off to do this work."

Suddenly I felt like Toto in *The Wizard of Oz* when Dorothy exclaims, "Run, Toto, run."

I was out of there in a hurry.

The only other incident where I thought I might be dealing with a charlatan occurred near La Jolla, California, early in my journey. I was attending a wedding scheduled for late afternoon on a Saturday, and the hotel where guests were booked was close to the beach. I took a long, fast walk on the sand early that morning and eventually wound my way back into the quaint town. Now meandering along the pretty streets, I came upon a sign, more of a shingle really, that said, READER AND ADVISOR: TAROT CARDS AND PALM READING. I had time to kill and I thought, *This could be educational.* I followed the path around the small stucco house with the sign and knocked on the front door. A plainly dressed, pleasant woman with wavy dark hair answered the door and invited me into what appeared to be her living room. There was a large floor-to-ceiling bay window in the front, and I had a clear view of the street, so I felt I could relax. We sat facing each other, with her on a small love seat and me in a comfortable side chair. She immediately explained the price she charged for the tarot card reading and the price of the palm reading. I said I'd like the tarot card reading and paid her $25. I wasn't really interested in the reading. I was just curious about how she conducted her business, how she presented herself to the public. She read the cards, and nothing she said resonated. Nothing. I don't even remember what she said. What I do remember is that when we ended the half-hour session, she said, "I can tell you more [about whatever she had told me that was meaningless] if you pay me more." And the "more" was double the half-hour charge. I couldn't wait to get out of there.

I decided that from that point on, I would work with or meet with only someone recommended by a person I knew well and, more important, someone I trusted and respected.

That's how I found Stephen Barr, a professional who was of Robin's caliber. I was introduced to him by a friend whose judgment and intellect I admired and who demonstrated, more than anyone I was close to at that time, a sophisticated appreciation of the higher realm. I talked to her about some of my experiences, carefully avoiding too much detail. I wanted to tread lightly so that she could easily refrain from discussing anything if she felt at all uncomfortable. Fortunately, she immediately understood. She recommended that I make an appointment with Stephen, who had been extremely helpful to both her and her husband.

I drove to Tahoe City to meet with Stephen at his Healing Arts Center in the summer of 2005 for the first of what would be five visits over seven years. Stephen is a handsome, lean, tall man with thick silver-gray hair that reflects his wisdom more than his age (early sixties). With crystal-clear aqua-blue eyes, he is a very healthy man, but beyond his physical presence, he has an aura that suggests an old soul. He is soft-spoken and immediately made me feel safe and at ease.

Stephen seems to defy the classic division between left-brain analysis and right-brain creativity: he is a spiritual healer grounded in the hard sciences. Born in Cincinnati in 1948, he was always told he was too serious and too sensitive when he was growing up. He seemed to know what people were feeling but was chastised when he mentioned it, so he shut it down.

Seeking a less conservative environment, he left town to go to the Massachusetts Institute of Technology, where he graduated with a bachelor's degree in electrical engineering in 1970.

He joined the Peace Corps and taught math and science in Nepal. The only Westerner in a village with no roads, toilets, or running water, he was struck by the realization that the people were poor but happy. During his second year, his girlfriend, later his wife, arrived in a Volkswagen Squareback that she had driven from Germany. Together they drove the car through Nepal, India, Pakistan, Afghanistan, and Europe, the ultimate road trip, which would be close to impossible today.

During the long hours of traveling, Stephen was reading Eastern philosophy and planning his future. Practicality beckoned. On his return to the United States, he took a job with a company making biofeedback mechanisms for consumers. It was a small company, so he wore many hats, including those of circuit designer and tester, and the easiest person to use for testing was, of course, himself. Because the product he was testing measured brain waves, he had stumbled onto the bridge between electrical engineering and meditation.

Interest in meditation trumped interest in circuit design, so he and his wife enrolled in the Arica School, which, unlike some of the ancient schools of meditation and enlightenment, uses contemporary methods of biology, psychology, and physics to clarify human consciousness. At Arica, Stephen learned different types of meditation, massage, and spiritual work involving karma. He graduated, and then he taught there for several years.

Later a friend of Stephen's was leaving for acupuncture school in England, so he decided to go with her. It was there, under the instruction of clairvoyant Professor J. R. Worsley, that he learned the mental and spiritual side of acupuncture.

He ultimately moved to Lake Tahoe, California, to begin an internship with Jeffrey Kauffman, a medical doctor who incorporates holistic approaches into his practice. It didn't take long to learn that Lake Tahoe in those days was a far cry from Boston and might not meet Stephen's needs for culture and spiritual community. So he moved to Marin County and faced more frustrations. Nothing seemed to be working.

Then a friend without a car asked him to drive her to Lake Tahoe. During the trip, he heard the inner voice for the first time, a booming *Yes*. This time he decided to stay in Lake Tahoe, and he has been there for more than thirty-five years.

He says he's not leaving until the voice that guided him there tells him to leave.

A Course in Miracles, by Helen Schucman and William Thetford, offers practical lessons and applications for the practice of forgiveness, and the book has profoundly impacted Stephen. He describes it as a mental path. The workbook is extensive, more than twelve hundred pages, and Stephen has completed it several times. He heard the inner voice a second time, and he and his wife started and led a group dedicated to the book for more than four years. One of the things *A Course in Miracles* taught him was that the truth is unequivocal. As he puts it, "When something has the ring of truth, it silences the arguments."

He heard the inner voice while he was treating a client who was about to leave for India to join her guru, convert to Hinduism, and shave her head so she would be allowed in the temples. The voice said, *Give her some money.* He had only $10 in his wallet, but he gave it to her for offerings. Stephen and his wife had been trying to have a child and conceived their daughter on January 21. When the client came back from India, he asked her where she had been on January 21, and she told him she had made his offering at her first temple, built in honor of Shakti, the female consort of Shiva, a Hindu deity.

Like Robin, Stephen believes that the spirit world coexists with this world. He believes that spirits visited me just as they visit many people who are open and receptive. Stephen doesn't necessarily think it was Max's handprint on the mirror, but he does believe the handprint came from another dimension. Stephen also told me that in a previous life I had an unresolved issue over not being able to say good-bye to a husband before he died. "Perhaps," Stephen reasoned, "that provoked these activities."

On my initial visit he found that my aura—a luminous field that surrounds each person and is visible to some people— extended more than the normal three to five feet. Stephen's process to help someone with this situation is to call in the Divine Powers, or guides, to help him clear the spiritual space and emotional levels of his clients. He did this for me, and he has done it for many of his clients. It's not unusual to need this clearing when you're going through grief.

On another visit, Stephen gave me a mantra to use whenever I felt I needed it. It is a Tibetan mantra called the Vajra Guru Mantra: *om ah hum vajra guru padma siddhi hum*. Reciting the mantra purifies the body and surrounding environment, removing obstacles such as ill health and supporting positive aspirations such as prosperity and long life, he explained. The mantra also encourages spiritual practice. I had never had a mantra before and felt a little self-conscious saying it out loud. But I got over being timid when I found it was genuinely soothing.

I asked Stephen to tell me more about the guides and how they work. "Is it always the same guides?" I asked.

"No," he said, "there seems to be a number of guides assigned to all of us. It's like a committee, but the membership of the committee rotates as we learn our life lessons. But it's usually about five to eight guides."

I asked if the guides have gender. "No," Stephen said, "they are fairly androgynous."

"Where are they?" I asked.

Stephen said, "We're trapped in three dimensions plus time. The guides are not in that box. They are beyond time and space."

I asked Stephen to tell me the most important thing I

should know about the guides. Intriguingly, he said, "The guides tell me they would like to give us more help than we ask for. But they can't intervene and impose their wishes without our requests because we have free will. Don't hesitate to ask for help. Nothing is too large or too small, and we have to invite the help. The guides won't intervene unless invited."

Stephen, like Robin, was a great help in expanding my thinking and assisting my growth. I am grateful to both.

CHAPTER 7

A Pattern Emerges

I went to work with a heavy heart on Monday, May 8, 2006, the second anniversary of Max's death. Thank goodness for *The Sacramento Bee*. It was a godsend in every sense of the word. I loved my job and especially the people at *The Bee*. I knew it was going to be a trying and sad twenty-four hours, but I was focused on the routine at the paper and was consumed by the work throughout the day.

Around seven p.m. I returned home. Tanner was at his dad's house that evening. I entered our home through the garage as I usually did. Coming into the house this way required me to pass by the bathroom that Max had used—the same bathroom where Tanner and I had seen the handprint exactly one year before. Naturally, I had to look. My mind said, *This surely wouldn't happen again. Not a second time. Not possible.*

I looked. I was blown away.

The mirror once again held images, this time in somewhat indistinguishable form. They consisted of the same powdery substance as the earlier ones. I quickly grabbed my camera and took photos. As I faced the mirror, the largest image on my right looked like an angel in a shape similar to those that top a Christmas tree, with perfectly formed wings sticking out on the side. It looked graceful and pretty. In the middle, slightly higher, was a small image shaped like a "baby" angel with open wings that gave the appearance of fluttering. Up higher on my left was a third image that looked like a bird with a small round beak.

I knew the powdery images were real even if I wasn't certain what they were. And I also knew this now represented a pattern. Both times, the images had occurred on the anniversary of Max's death. I was torn. Part of me wanted to keep them on the mirror. After all, how could I turn my back on them—or on him, if it was Max? But I also knew it had been two years since Max had died, and I had made some progress getting on with my life.

I left the powdery images there on Monday and Tuesday. I showed them to Helen on Wednesday morning, and her perception was different. She thought they looked like a person was cupping their hands in a C shape against the mirror to shield their eyes as they placed their face against the mirror, perhaps from the other side. But she also acknowledged that two of the images could be perceived as angels. Before leaving the house that morning, I washed them off with Windex myself. I knew that something miraculous was occurring, but I remained uncertain as to what I should do about it.

Soon I would meet someone who would help me move forward, on many levels.

In the summer that followed the second set of anniversary images, I began to consider that I might want to date again. I think any woman who has started the dating game in her fifties would agree with me—this is not fun or easy. No. On the contrary, it's scary and difficult. But I missed male companionship, and going solo to events was always a reminder that I was—yes, solo. So I decided to plunge ahead, asking a few of my friends if they knew of anyone they might introduce me to. Guess what? They did.

In one instance I was informally introduced to a "prospect" by a friend of a friend. "Just check him out," she said. "And if you like what you see and learn, I'll put it together."

So off we drove to a casual dinner party in San Francisco, where I was to "observe the prospect." My prospect looked very much like a baked potato with loafers sticking out at the bottom. Not that I'm any prize, and not that looks are all that matter. But there has to be some basis of attraction, right?

After that I was a bit reticent, until one of my friends brought up Jim Durham, a man I actually knew. More than one friend told me that Jim and his wife had separated and were getting divorced. They said that he was an impressive guy. He's smart and successful, loves to read, has two really neat sons, and is a big outdoorsman, my friends told me.

Oh, and he's handsome, they added. That part I was aware of. Max and I had known both Jim and his wife casually. We would often see them and her family at various Sacramento community events. Occasionally, Max, Tanner, and I would run into them at a local restaurant and stop to chat.

With my friends giving me encouragement, I called Jim. I told him that Tanner, a junior in high school, was looking at colleges in the East as well as in California. I knew that both of Jim's sons had gone to East Coast universities after graduating from high school in California, and I asked if he could give me advice about whether that would be a worthwhile option for

Tanner to consider. We talked for about half an hour, and he was very friendly and helpful. I took notes. But it wasn't until the end of the conversation that he gave me the most critical piece of information. He told me about his divorce.

This was my opening. Later Jim would tell me that I'm one of the best "fly fishermen" he's ever known, carefully presenting the fly (me) in front of an unsuspecting trout (him), then setting the hook.

I asked him during our phone call if he remembered Tanner, who had been ten years old the last time Jim had seen him. "Would you like to see a picture of the young man he has grown into?" I asked. "Of course I would," Jim responded.

A few weeks earlier, one of The Bee's photographers had taken a picture of Tanner and me at a Sacramento Kings basketball game. Tanner, on the cusp of turning sixteen, had grown into a very handsome young man. I was seated next to him. No woman likes to see herself up close in a mirror or a photograph after a certain fifty-something age, but this photo miraculously highlighted what remaining assets I had! (It's amazing what those professional photographers with their fancy cameras can do.)

I sent the photo to Jim. Two weeks later, he called me for dinner. It was a perfect cast, and the trout was on.

I never thought I would find true love again. But Max had predicted that not only would I fall in love again; I'd be happier than ever before, because, as he put it, "I will be there with you." I took that to mean that our love would endure, even after his death. I didn't realize that perhaps he meant that our love would change me and make me open to love again.

When I met Jim for our first dinner date at Piatti restaurant near my home in Sacramento in the summer of 2006, I felt an immense attraction to him from the beginning. The chemistry between us was electric. And that's quite a gift. I believe it's either there or it's not. You can't work to invent it.

I fell in love with Jim easily and naturally and have remained hopelessly in love ever since. I have often been asked by close friends how I reconciled the love I had for Max with the new love I discovered with Jim. They wondered if I let go of loving Max to be free to love Jim. "What does it say about you that you fell so hard for Jim when you were so in love with Max, who has only been gone for a little over two years now?" Fair questions.

During those first months after Max died, I saw a grief counselor. She told me there's an old adage that "women grieve, men replace" after the death of a spouse. I don't know what I was supposed to do or what society measures as the norm. I only know what my heart told me then and now. I believe love is infinite and unlimited. Your heart doesn't divide. It multiplies. And if you are lucky enough to find love again, there is no option other than to go for it. Isn't that what we live for?

From that first dinner on, we were together whenever possible. Jim lived part-time in Sun Valley, Idaho, and part-time in Dallas, where he was CEO of a company he had founded three years earlier. I was buried in my responsibilities at *The Bee*. Jim also was making the trip from Idaho to California every other weekend, sometimes more. We would spend time in both Sacramento and Yountville enjoying friends and family.

Best of all, Jim made me laugh again in a way I had forgotten over the previous two years. As the Reverend Jesse Vaughan said to Jim when they met, "You put the light back in Janis's eyes." And, indeed, he had.

As the prospects for our new life were beginning to coalesce, the extraordinary events continued. Jim and I spoke regularly over the phone. One night I took his call on the line in the bedroom, but the phone fell silent within a minute. Jim called back, and I answered on the same phone. Shortly thereafter it went silent again. Jim fortunately called back, and this time I answered on the phone in the kitchen. The connection dropped again. The next morning Jim called me at the office saying he'd had no problems with his phone and wondered if there was an issue with mine. I called Pacific Bell to have them check the phones at my home. I drove home to meet them there while they inspected the entire system. They said they could find nothing wrong.

One of the many things that Jim and I share is a passion for Napa Valley. On a spectacular fall weekend, he suggested we drive to Napa to hike and relax. He was driving us north on Highway 29 in his car on the way to St. Helena from Yountville. I noticed a hotel on the left as we were entering St. Helena and told Jim that was where Max often stayed in Napa before he met me. Max loved the place for its simplicity and location. As we passed it, Jim's car radio suddenly came on loudly out of the clear blue. He seemed surprised and fumbled around trying to find the cause. Finally he just turned it off. We looked at each other as if to say, *Well, that was weird.*

On the way back to Yountville, we passed the same hotel. The radio came on again. This time we said what we were thinking. "How did that happen? What are the probabilities?" When Jim returned to Sun Valley, he took his car to the dealer to have the radio checked. The service manager told Jim he had never heard of such a thing and determined that the radio was fine.

When I first told Jim about the events that followed

Max's death, I was very nervous. Not surprisingly, I was concerned that he would think the woman he had been dating for six months was a fruitcake. It was only rational to be concerned. Jim has an undergraduate degree in engineering from the University of Florida (Go, Gators!) and an MBA specializing in finance from UCLA (Go, Bruins!). He is also a CPA as well as a CEO. In short, he is the last person to buy into something that isn't objective and quantifiable. When I first told him the stories and showed him some of the photographs, he didn't disappoint.

He said, "It sounds a little woo-woo to me." But at least he kept calling.

He knew I was worried that he would think I was a nutcase. He had never experienced or focused on anything this unusual, but "I was open to it," he told me later.

I think it was helpful that Jim had known Max casually and had a great deal of respect for him. Jim hadn't engaged in long conversations with Max, but he felt that he had a sense of Max as a man and always liked him.

These two men were remarkably alike. Jim, like Max, is a smart, kind, thoughtful, passionate, and loving man. He is the strongest man I have ever known. I've never seen him afraid of anything (well, except for my cooking, maybe).

Jim loves classical music and introduced me to one of his passions, the Sun Valley Summer Symphony. He is an opera lover and once played a role as a supernumerary in a San Francisco Opera production of *Aida*. He also loves wine and has assembled an impressive collection in his cellar in Sun Valley. And he reads books—lots of them and all the time. He reads almost exclusively nonfiction, much of it religion. But he's not entirely like Max. Jim has a black belt in tae kwon do, is an avid fisherman, hunter, and sailor, and loves to hike in the mountains around Sun Valley.

In October 2007 Jim invited me to Sun Valley for my birthday and threw me a surprise party, where I met some of his best friends. It didn't take long for me to fall in love with Sun Valley. One beautiful fall day, we were hiking the nearby Baker Lake trailhead, enjoying the gorgeous canyons, the rambling creeks, and the breathtaking vistas, when Jim surprised me with a question that never would have entered my mind.

"Why don't you consider retiring?" he said.

I stopped still in my tracks. The wind was blowing softly through the aspen and pine trees, and I could feel my heart thumping in my chest. I stared down at my hiking shoes for a minute before looking back up and meeting Jim's eyes.

"How can I quit working? Working is what I do. It's what I've always done," I replied defensively. Clearly, I was clinging to my job because it was something stable that I didn't have to change when change was all I had done since Max died and I struggled to stay afloat. But I was wrong about change. Change was the path to my spiritual growth, and avoiding it was impossible.

CHAPTER 8

Is Max Trying to Reach Me?

Running a newspaper in 2007 meant unprecedented challenges, with the economy in decline and Internet competitors eroding our advertising. We were downsizing and with that came the inevitable layoffs, affecting people's lives in painful ways.

Fortunately, the McClatchy Company and by extension *The Sacramento Bee* were thoughtful and cautious about the process. McClatchy was known to have a tradition of concern for employees and for treating them fairly. I felt grateful to work in a culture where character and values mattered. I was confident that we would make any tough decisions with compassion and generosity.

On February 21, one day before Jim's birthday, my father died at the age of eighty-nine. He had been suffering from prostate cancer for a few years, and now, sadly, it had metastasized throughout his body. He was in severe pain. We'd known he didn't have much time left, so my brother Kurt and I flew to McCook, Nebraska, to be with both Mom and Dad and to say good-bye to him. My brother Brian and sister Signe came shortly after to pay their respects as well. It was the last time we would see him. He died shortly after our visit.

When Kurt and I arrived at the independent living facility where Mom and Dad were living, I found myself as worried about Mom as I was about Dad. This was highly unusual for me. For most of my life it was Dad whom I thought of first and whom I cared and worried about most. What was this unfamiliar concern I had for Mom? Perhaps it was genuine empathy. For the first time I knew exactly how she felt. I knew what she was going through watching him slowly die, what she would be facing the day he died, and what she would be in for over the next months and years. Maybe, just maybe, for once I could help.

Mom answered the door, clearly relieved to see us. She wept slightly when she gave us a hug, and I could sense that she was frazzled and distraught. We were anxious to see Dad so we immediately headed to his bedroom. There he was, weakened and frail, faded almost, sleeping quietly. The outline of his shrunken body beneath the sheets made me gasp. It was so reminiscent of Max in his final days. I hated seeing Dad like this just as I'd hated seeing Max like this. But at least Dad had enjoyed a full life instead of being cut down at the age of fifty-six. As painful as it is, we are expected to be witness to the death of our parents. It's natural. Premature death is not.

Kurt and I chose to let Dad sleep and tiptoed back out to the living room to talk to Mom. As Mom and Kurt began discussing hospice arrangements, I found myself surveying their small apartment. Things looked pretty chaotic. There were open boxes with books next to miscellaneous papers and newspaper articles stacked high and without any apparent order. Family photographs were in small and large boxes on tables and counters, leaving not a shred of space for much of anything else. The apartment was practically claustrophobic.

Out of the corner of my eye, something caught my attention. It was a medium-size cardboard box on the floor in the dining room next to the table. Something green and red was sticking out of it. Walking over, I sat down in a chair to peer into the box. And that's when I saw it. It was the hideous Christmas ornament that we had when the kids all lived at home in the fifties. I think Mom and Dad bought it at a church rummage sale. It was made of about a dozen four-inch clear plastic cups that mimicked small shades on a chandelier and was loosely strung together by a thin, waxy, straw rope. Intertwined in a frenetic fashion were two strings of Christmas lights, one green and one red, the wires all tangled and the bulbs sticking out haphazardly. *What in the world is this of all things doing in the dining room?* I thought. I sat back in the chair and took a deep breath. *It's not the plastic that she's holding on to; it's the Christmas memories.* I felt a tug in my heart.

But the tug didn't last long. The spell was broken as I heard Mom, with her loud, shrill voice, getting agitated. She was talking animatedly to Kurt, not noticing or caring when he tried to interject something, which was typical. She was expressing some criticism she had regarding the weight of what she perceived to be a rather large hospice worker who had visited the day before.

"I don't understand where they get these people," she said. "How could they let her be so heavy and come over here? How is she going to help us if she can't move around the apartment?"

Never mind that Twiggy would have had trouble finessing her way around this teensy apartment jammed full of memorabilia. It was an obstacle course. *Why is Mom always so critical? Why can't she just appreciate the wonderful services that hospice personnel provide?*

I couldn't help myself. I was slipping back into old habits, being disappointed in Mom instead of helping her when she needed me most. I told myself to snap out of it. I knew that this particular moment in time mattered—really mattered—because I had been through it myself and I understood that I could not have made it without the support of loved ones.

Mom was more high-strung and hyper than ever. Who wouldn't be? She was under immense pressure to cope not only with Dad's impending death, but also with the details of managing his care in the interim. I went to the couch and sat down to share in the conversation. Yes, there was a part of me that wished I had earplugs, but the mature part of me engaged, and together the three of us began to make a plan.

Later that evening, Dad woke up and was able to join us in the living room. As he slowly shuffled into the room in his pajamas and slippers, I stared at his balding head and hunched shoulders. He was razor thin, feeble, and diminished. He had no color in his face, and his eyes looked blank, detached. I recognized this condition all too well. The cancer and painkillers had robbed him the way they robbed Max. Only a fragment of the real him was present. And at that exact moment, I knew that the last time I would have a meaningful conversation with him had already passed.

As he settled into his recliner, it hit me that he would never know about the handprint. I had flubbed it. I had taken too long to bring it to him. Dealing with my grief and suppressing the events had taken precedence over sharing it with him or anyone those first years. Then Dad got sick with cancer, and I didn't want to risk upsetting or worrying him in any way. Now his illness had gone too far and it was too late.

We spent our time that night talking about details associated with the practical aspects of his impending death. Dad was insistent on filling us in on his pension, even though that topic had already been addressed. He reiterated his concerns about where Mom would live, even though that had all been settled. He was worried about the boxes (yes, more boxes) in storage and how we were going to pull them together for Mom.

I couldn't help but be disappointed. The Dad I had known wasn't the Dad we were witnessing tonight. And then I remembered it was similar with Max. Max was only vaguely himself in the last few days before he died. Just like Dad now, he didn't seem all there. But Tanner and I treated Max as if he were with us until the very end. Now Kurt, Mom, and I needed to behave the same with Dad. And we did. We let him hold forth however he desired on whatever topics he chose. It was the last thing we were able to give to him. We promised we would handle whatever was necessary with Mom, and he seemed relieved.

During those next few days Dad mostly slept. Mom didn't. The quieter he became, the more exaggerated her personality seemed. And I don't mean in a particularly positive way. This dynamic was not uncharacteristic of what was now a nearly six-decade-long pattern. But I began to detect a tiny crack in the plaster when I realized I was actually coping with the situation. Instead of freaking out and pitching a tent on my side of every topic we discussed, I stepped back and gave her room. It didn't matter if the boxes were everywhere, tripping us on a regular basis. Who cared? They were her boxes. It was her home. She was losing her husband. I "parked a bus on my lip," as one of my astute twelve-year-old students once recommended that his reading partner do back in Seven Mile, Ohio. My observations were still in my head, but instead of leaking out, they stayed put. Now was not the time to fight. Far from it. I knew all too well the agony, the fear, the anguish she was experiencing.

The day we left, both Kurt and I quietly entered Dad's bedroom to say good-bye for what we knew would be the last time. Standing behind Kurt as he bent over to kiss Dad on the cheek, I noticed that his hands were identical to our dad's. Kurt, who has a huge heart, was struggling with his emotions; the pain he was feeling was palpable. He told Dad he loved him and slowly backed out of the way. I stepped into the space he left and knelt down to say my farewells. I noticed Mom in the corner crying. It struck me that her ordinary demonstrative show of emotions was taking a backseat to a far more reserved self. Turning my attention back to Dad, I kissed him and told him I loved him. What else is there to do when someone you love is going to die? It's all that's left to say, to do. It's a privilege. And it's over in an instant.

Later that morning, Kurt and I flew back home separately. He went to Seattle, and I flew to Sacramento. The plane ride afforded much-needed time to reflect on what had just happened. I thought about Dad not just as he was on this trip, sick and absent, but as he'd been for most of my life. I reminisced about our conversations, the connection we shared, and the example he had set. I knew that the love he felt for his family was the foundation of our lives as we had grown from children to adults. It's what we pass on to our children. How do you value that? It's everything.

And so I felt flooded with a sense of gratitude, not sadness.

I thought it a bit strange that I wasn't more sad. Maybe it was because Dad was eighty-nine and had lived a full and long life. Or was it possible that because of what I had experienced with Max, I could now deal with Dad's death more positively? My convictions about death were shifting. I was realizing (yet again) the power of love. How could a love so strong do anything but live on? Is it possible that the web of unconditional love we experience in life extends beyond our human realm and that the spirit or soul is a manifestation of that love? I was gaining confidence that love is the key to what matters most in life.

About a month after Dad died I had a vivid dream, or maybe it was a visit from him. I'm not sure. I woke up in the middle of the night, and he was sitting in a metal folding chair at the foot of my bed. He had his legs crossed and he was handsome and strong again, as he was when I was a girl. He was wearing a dark black suit with a crisp white shirt and bright tie. He didn't speak. He just looked at me and smiled. His eyes and mine locked. What I heard, though not from a voice, was *I'm okay*. Then he disappeared.

Just as Max had credited family and loved ones with carrying him through the darkest time of his life, so it was family and loved ones who carried me through the challenges in 2007. The two brightest spots in my life were Tanner and Jim. I don't know what I would have done without them. Jim and I saw each other regularly and spoke on the phone every night when we weren't together.

We were beginning to talk around the edges of a serious commitment. At least that's my story. As Jim puts it, I was working up to announcing that we were getting married. And I thought a "five-year plan" might be in order. Seriously, I did present one to him at Campton Place in San Francisco one night at the bar. He was speechless. But that's another story.

Yet Max still seemed to be in my life. Was it possible that Max was trapped and couldn't move on? I had heard that sometimes a very strong love could prevent a spirit from leaving the person they love and moving forward to the light. The house phone (the same one Pacific Bell pronounced as working perfectly) would still go out once in a while when Jim and I were talking long-distance. When we were together, the lights continued to flicker. It was hard not to surmise it was Max.

Jim was now witnessing all of these phenomena. One weekend when we were in Yountville, I got a call from the alarm company telling me that the motion detector in my Sacramento home had been triggered. The windows and doors had not been opened. The alarm company reps said no one had entered the house, but "something" was in the hallway to activate it. I knew there was no one in the house, since Tanner was out of town at a rugby game that weekend with his teammates. Maybe it was a system failure (although when the alarm company checked it later, no problem was found). But it was odd because the motion detector was in the hall outside my bedroom. More significant, this happened on the date Max and I had married seven years earlier.

And the golden threads revisited me. One morning I got into my car in the garage, ready to leave for work, and my windshield was covered with the same golden "corn silk" threads I had seen in the bathtub. Only this time they were everywhere. There must have been fifty of them. And just as before, when I touched them they disappeared.

I could now share these events with Jim, and I was learning that things I once considered unbelievable were believable because they were real. I wasn't scared and Jim wasn't either. Occasionally he found the events frustrating, but mostly he was fascinated and increasingly curious.

On Saturday, May 5, 2007, a good friend and her husband invited Tanner and me over to their home for a casual dinner. They were aware that the third anniversary of Max's passing was approaching on May 8 and they knew Jim was out of town, so they had extended the offer as a thoughtful gesture.

I had worn Max's wedding band on a silver chain around my neck every day for the year following his death. On the first anniversary of his death, it seemed fitting to take if off and keep it permanently in my jewelry box. But for whatever reason, this particular Saturday evening, I pulled it from my jewelry box and wore it once again. When I came home from our dinner I forgot to take it off and wore it to bed. The next morning I was preparing breakfast for Tanner, and I went into the guest bathroom (yes, that one) because it was off the kitchen.

Unbelievable! It was happening again!

This time the handprint was a left hand, as opposed to the right hand Tanner and I had seen on the first anniversary of Max's death. And it was much larger than the already quite sizable hand of 2005. The palm portion was heftier, with the fingers seemingly amorphous, not as controlled or defined as the first X-ray-like image in 2005.

Now the fingers tapered to a point that extended farther out than fingers normally would. To me, it looked as if energy was flowing out of the fingertips. This handprint felt as if it could be a progression, or gradual loss of form, compared with the first handprint. Perhaps, if this was Max, he was changing. Along with the hand were what seemed to be fragments of wings, similar to what I'd seen on the images of angels in 2006.

The prints appeared to be of the same powdery substance as the other images.

Just as I was when I discovered the hand on the mirror in 2005 and the angels in 2006, I was stunned initially. But I was less shocked because it was the third time. I was becoming less frightened, more inquisitive, more accepting. Instead of crying out hysterically for Tanner to come into the bathroom, I calmly walked back out to the kitchen, where Tanner was seated at the table reading the sports section of *The Bee,* to tell him about it.

"You're not going to believe this, Tanner."

"What, Mom?" he answered without looking up. (At the time he was seventeen, not the fifteen-year-old he was the first time we saw the image.)

"It's back. The hand on the mirror is back. Only it's larger and...and..."

Tanner wasn't waiting for me to finish. He bolted from his chair and walked the few paces to the bathroom. I followed directly behind him, but he had grown so much that his body blocked the doorway into the bathroom. So I couldn't see his expression at first. Then he turned back around to face me. He was clearly taken aback.

"Mom, it's not possible. I don't get it. Do you think it's Max since it's only a couple days before May 8? What do you think he's trying to tell us? Is he lost?"

"I wish I knew the answer. I don't. But I suspect it's him and he wants us to know that he's still around. What do you think of the hand compared to the time we first saw it?"

"Well, it's way different. The palm is a lot bigger. And the fingers look like tiny flames from a birthday candle. The other time it looked more like a real hand."

"Yes, and it's the left hand this time," I added.

"I wonder how Max is able to make the powdery stuff, Mom. If he's doing it from heaven, how does he do it?"

"I don't know, Tanner. I'm stumped too. But let's eat our breakfast and we can talk more then."

We sat down to muffins, fruit, and eggs and continued our discussion. Neither Tanner nor I was afraid; rather, we were mystified and curious. We talked about how this was the third time images had spontaneously appeared on or near the anniversary of Max's passing. Denying that a pattern existed was ignoring reality. This was real, and we knew it because we'd witnessed it. I explained to Tanner that we would go on with our lives and that sometimes living with ambiguity is necessary in a world that can be complicated. We agreed that we both trusted Max and that someday we'd understand. But for now we would just trust.

After breakfast, Tanner and I examined the print again. I took photos and decided to leave the imprints on the mirror when I left for work and Tanner went to school on Monday morning. After I got home that evening, the images were still there. I took more photos. On Tuesday, May 8, the anniversary of Max's death, the images were unchanged.

A day or so later I rubbed the images off the mirror. How could it be an accident that this happened again around the anniversary of Max's death? I decided to call Robin.

She continued to believe that it was Max leaving the images and that he was not moving on. She suggested I try something called smudging. I didn't know what that was, so she explained that smudging involves burning sage in the bathroom where I was seeing the images. The idea is based on ancient healing rituals, including Native American spiritual practices. She also told me to walk the perimeter of my house ringing a bell and inviting Max to move on and go to the light, where he belonged. So I called a friend who was spiritually oriented and asked her if she would be willing to assist me. I had no idea how to do this.

My friend told me to go buy some sage and said that she would be over soon. When she arrived, she started laughing. "Not that kind of sage," she said. I had gone to the spices aisle at Raley's grocery store and purchased a bottle of dried sage. Apparently, I was supposed to go to a New Age store, where they sell it in sticks. Who knew?

Anyway, we marched around the perimeter of the house ringing a bell and suggesting to Max that he would be happy once he settled into heaven or the spirit world. We looked more than a little silly. I was trying to be a trouper, but I was preoccupied with the idea that we might be discovered. Thankfully our neighbors weren't home.

Robin also suggested that Jim speak to Max and tell him it was okay to move on to the spirit world. Since I was committed to helping Max in any way possible, I asked Jim if he would. To his credit, he did it, and he did it with grace. He said he felt a little foolish, but he was also beginning to believe in the idea that there was more than our physical selves, so he was open to trying to reach out to this other dimension.

"It's time for you to move on to the next stage, Max. This is your destiny. You don't have to worry about Janis. I will take care of her," he said in front of the bathroom mirror where the handprints had appeared.

In spite of a thirty-year career that regularly called on my natural skepticism, I had learned from my father to keep an open mind to all possibilities. And I'm glad I did. Because Robin's recommendations seemed to work. After the summer of

2007, no more images appeared, no more lights flickered, and no more clocks stopped at my home in Sacramento. It was over, at least at that location.

Fortunately, 2007 would bring exciting, happy events that helped offset the challenges of these otherworldly happenings. In late May I had the honor and privilege to go to Columbia University in New York City, along with Renée Byer and other *Sacramento Bee* employees, to watch Renée receive the Pulitzer Prize for feature photography for her work in *A Mother's Journey*, a series that chronicled the final days of a young boy dying of cancer. The last time I had been at Columbia was in 2005 to watch *Bee* editorial writer Tom Philp receive the Pulitzer for his editorial series on the restoration of Hetch Hetchy Valley in Yosemite National Park. As I glanced around our table of *Bee* journalists, I could not help thinking of those individuals who were no longer with us. We owed them for the rich journalistic legacy they left us, a legacy that was clearly dynamic, not static. In other words, even though our predecessors from decades earlier were departed, their essence remained and was a source of inspiration to all of us.

Jim, a voracious reader, was excited when I invited him to join me at Columbia for the ceremony. He sat beside me at the luncheon with everyone else and was clearly engaged and enjoying himself. I was incredibly happy to have him with me to share in the moment.

Probably correlated with his appetite for reading is the fact that Jim is quite intelligent. But, let's face it, he is a male and therefore vulnerable to blind spots. One Sunday morning after we got back from New York, we were enjoying our standard breakfast smoothies and coffee in the kitchen in Sacramento while reading *The Bee*. We were both in a good mood. I thought it might be an opportune time to gently slip in a question about our future while he was relaxed and a bit distracted.

"So what do you see as a future for our relationship?" I asked in the same manner you would ask about the weather. "Do you have a plan?" (I'm imagining something like naming an engagement date, planning a wedding date, and nailing it down.)

It was as if I were talking to an alien from outer space. He looked up from the paper, not fully grasping what was happening to him, and said, "Well, I was thinking maybe we would live together and then after a few years we'll talk and decide where to go from there."

There was a long pause, during which I could tell that he was wondering if he should have given more thought to his answer. Finally I replied, "So that's your plan?"

As a sailor, Jim was now realizing that he was headed for turbulent waters but couldn't turn the boat around.

So after another long pause he said, "Well...yeah."

To which I took one nanosecond to reply with what any female in her right mind would say: "Well, your plan sucks." But I had a smile on my face.

We laughed out loud, and we still laugh about it today. Best of all, he changed his plan. In the fall, Jim finally came to his senses and asked me to marry him.

CHAPTER 9

Milestones

In April 2008, I retired from *The Sacramento Bee*. Jim's suggestion on our Sun Valley hike to Baker Lake in the fall of 2007 had seemed cockamamie, but it wasn't. It was brilliant. Now I would be able to devote myself to connecting the dots, in hopes of finding a way to make sense of the phenomena that had occurred since Max died. Best of all, I would have Jim by my side every day, a true partner, to bounce thoughts off of and to help me sort through a strategy. My desire to learn, to grow, to root myself in something spiritual, would have what it deserved: my full attention.

From a practical sense, the timing could not have been better. I was fifty-seven. Other than weekends and annual vacations, I'd been working pretty much every day for thirty-two years. I had saved a decent amount of the money I'd made over those years and had a pension from the McClatchy Company, so I could afford it. More important, Tanner was graduating from high school and was headed to the University of California,

Los Angeles. A whole new chapter of his life was about to begin. And Jim and I were getting married in July. We had decided to live in Sun Valley because we both loved the beauty and the lifestyle, hiking in the summers and skiing in the winters.

The love affair I had with the newspaper would never end. I missed my colleagues and friends from that era, and the years we spent together were some of the best of my life.

I appreciated those relationships and the work, but I didn't spend a lot of time looking back after I left. Close friends predicted I would be bored in retirement, with not enough to do. But later, those same friends said they were surprised at how quickly I adjusted. To be fair, only a few close friends knew the full extent of my goal to explore the afterlife.

It was simply a matter of perspective. I viewed my retirement not as leaving what I loved doing (which I clearly was), but rather as having the gift of time to explore the spiritual realm. Jim once told me that you don't really retire—you just redirect. I was shifting my interests and passions from the concrete, verifiable world of newspapers to the intangible, unprovable spirit world. It was the perfect time to go for it. There was so much to dig into and research.

In June I sold our family home in Sacramento. Even though I was looking forward to moving to Sun Valley, I had a hard time coming to terms with putting our home on the market. Tanner and I loved that home. It was not just a house. I was sensitive to all the history and memories we'd made over the last decade of living there. After all, Tanner had grown from child to young adult under this roof. As I was busy packing our belongings and running around town to help Tanner with preparations for UCLA, certain images involuntarily flashed through my mind.

Fun birthday parties by the pool. Kids with wide-open faces splashing and pinching one another in the hot Sacramento summer sun. Casey, tail wagging, knocking over the eight-foot Subway sandwich, mustard flying.

Thanksgiving dinner. The aroma of Max's brined and roasted turkey cooking away in our oven while his eccentric and tiny four-foot-ten-inch mother entertained us with her witty humor.

Decorating for Christmas. Bing Crosby in the background singing "Do You Hear What I Hear?" Max bound and determined to untangle the discombobulated twinkle lights so he could teach Tanner how to string them properly.

Routine school nights. Tanner concentrating on homework, seated at the dining room table, springing out of his chair with questions about history or Spanish. Max listening to Mahler and reading Umberto Eco's *The Name of the Rose*.

Our wedding reception. Big tent all aglow with tiny lights. Everyone we cared about together under it. Slow dancing with Tanner and Max in a three-way hug to Nat King Cole's "When I Fall in Love," followed by a herd of bodies winding their way through a wild and crazy line dance. The Village People's "Y.M.C.A." blasting.

Max learning he was sick. Max fighting the cancer. Max losing the battle. Max saying good-bye to Tanner and me. Max dying. In our living room.

I raised my son and lost my husband here. My perspective of life and death was shifting as a result of Max's passing and the extraordinary events that unfolded afterward. How could leaving not hurt? I was emotionally attached on a very deep level to everything that had gone on in this home. Tanner was not exempt, either. It was painful for both of us. We talked about it, and he acknowledged he wished we didn't have to leave, but he understood that I wanted to start a new life with Jim in Sun Valley. He was, fortunately, focused on his future at college. And I'm sure he was enthusiastic about joining us for the skiing in the winter and fly-fishing in the summer.

I wondered about the spirit world events and whether they would continue in Sun Valley. Nothing had transpired in Sacramento since the powdery handprint on the third anniversary of Max's death in May 2007, yet other things had happened in Napa. It seemed that whatever was being revealed had to do with me, not the home.

I shipped our Sacramento belongings to Sun Valley, and Jim and I moved into a rental home while we waited on the completion of a new home he was building for us.

Finding love late in life is not always easy. And once you're in this new relationship, it's not exactly like the one you experienced when you were a spring chicken. Jim and I were the classic definition of "set in our ways." So living together under one roof meant learning to accommodate each other's habits and proclivities. This is particularly challenging when you are dealing with not only a sixty-one-year-old male, but a male who is both an engineer and a CPA. Things are supposed to be a certain way. And I don't mean sort of. (I, on the other hand, am entirely flexible and amenable.)

So after I had moved in with Jim, it was no surprise when he said to me one day in a "why are you bugging me?" tone of voice, "Why do you keep moving the rug in our bedroom?"

He was referring to an antique Persian rug I had brought from my Sacramento home. We had placed it at the foot of our bed over the top of the wall-to-wall carpet in our master bedroom. The rug was heavy, measuring five feet by seven feet, and it had taken the two of us to situate it initially. It wasn't intended to lay on carpet, but it added a needed touch of color to the otherwise monochromatic color scheme. And it fit perfectly, almost as if framed by the carpet underneath and beside it. We had positioned it between the foot of our bed and the hearth on the opposing wall. There was about a foot of space between the end of the bed and the edge of the rug, with the same amount on the other side relative to the fireplace.

Being the precise guy he is, and being the sailor he is, Jim likes things "squared away." He was apparently tired of getting down on his knees every day and dragging the rug back into place.

I had no clue what he was talking about. "I haven't ever moved it," I said.

"I don't get what's happening, then," he said.

I suggested he stop adjusting it every day, and together we decided to see what would happen. We checked it in the morning, and when we checked again that evening, the rug had moved eight inches away from the bed toward the hearth. Yes, that's right. The rug moved eight inches on its own. By itself. No one touched it. Eventually the edge of the rug moved far enough that it bumped into the base of the hearth. We assumed that would stop the movement. It didn't. The rug kept moving until its edge had curled up flush against the side of the hearth. Almost five inches of rug along the seven-foot perimeter was now perpendicular to the floor.

The entire incident was bizarre. Ludicrous. Yet we both witnessed it. We were shocked and astonished, stunned yet again.

"This makes no sense," Jim said, looking askance at the rug in its new position. "Rugs don't move on their own. They are inanimate objects. And there's no one in this house but us."

"I know. I know. You're right," I responded quickly. I sank into a soft club chair by the window to quietly catch my breath. Staring out through the glass, I let my mind work as I took in the view of the mountains. It was just like the first time I witnessed the handprint, in 2005. I was feeling a wide range of emotions simultaneously. Shock, skepticism, apprehension, awe. Then gradually, something that hadn't existed before began to resonate. It was a newly born acceptance. I was gaining confidence, and I wasn't as fearful, as skeptical, as before. After all, far too many things had happened since then. The misgivings I had harbored were still there, but they were shrinking. And replacing those dissolving doubts were a new trust and acceptance.

Standing up from the chair, I slowly walked over to Jim to hold his hand. I wanted the comfort and security of his strength. And I wanted to lend him some of my own. "We know this happened, and we experienced it together. Let's set the incident aside in our minds for now and move the rug upstairs to the office."

I knew we would get back to it when we had time after our wedding. The rug stayed put in its new room. But as it turned out, while we had seen the last of moving rugs in Sun Valley, we hadn't seen the last of them in Napa.

The day of our wedding finally arrived. We held a beautiful ceremony in mid-July on the lawn of a friend's home on the Big Wood River in Sun Valley. Across the river was the steep side of a mountain. Friends and family had come from all over the country to be with us, and our friend the Reverend Jesse Vaughan, the Episcopalian minister who had conducted Max's funeral, came from Sacramento to perform the ceremony. It simply couldn't have been any better. After dinner we were delighted to see a baby black bear come down the mountain on the other side of the river to see what we were up to. Bears are rare in the area, so to see one at the wedding was a treat for our guests. And our close friends know that my nickname for Jim is Bear.

We left for our honeymoon in Lake Louise and Banff, Canada, stopping on the way at Triple Creek Ranch in Montana. On Labor Day, we moved into our new home in Sun Valley. We were excited to begin our married life together. And I was eager to continue my journey of spiritual exploration with Jim by my side.

CHAPTER 10

Lessons from a Rocket Scientist

Jim was gradually coming to terms with these unusual events, but his acceptance came slowly. His skeptical attitude softened when he began to witness things firsthand.

Jim describes himself as agnostic. He doesn't subscribe to one particular religion and says he doesn't see God in the image of a man "sitting on a cloud." He does believe in a higher form of energy in the world. "Perhaps like gravity," he says, "invisible but definitely present." He feels it most keenly when he's in nature. Every time something unexplainable occurred, his approach to interpreting it was more clinical, more technical, than mine. He kept asking about energy fields. Wanting to understand these events from a scientific perspective, he was very curious as to whether energy might be playing a role. Of course, he was coming at it as an engineer and a CPA.

Although I was approaching my research from a more

spiritual standpoint, I was comfortable with the idea of exploring the role science might play. So having made the decision to include scientists along with spiritual practitioners, the question became—how?

One weekend in Sun Valley I saw a brochure at a local juice bar. (Just as I was making a habit of visiting alternative bookstores, I was now visiting juice bars and health food stores.) The brochure was for the Sun Valley Spiritual Film Festival, which explores spiritual traditions and celebrates them through film. The brochure promised film sessions, panel presentations, and speakers. I thought there might be a speaker or panelist there who could offer some insight into the realm of science relative to supernatural events. The location at the beautiful Sun Valley Lodge was a bonus.

After one particularly interesting film session in the old Opera House on the campus of the lodge, I approached one of the speakers. His company was in an alliance with leading academic institutions seeking to understand consciousness and the human energy field. A lot of people were milling around, so I had to wait my turn to talk to the presenter. I explained to him that unusual events had been occurring and I was seeking guidance on how to make sense of them. He seemed to be half listening until I mentioned the handprint.

Looking up from his notes, he said, "What did you say?"

"A handprint appeared on the mirror in my bathroom exactly one year after the death of my husband, who died in our home," I repeated.

"I have just the person you should meet," he said with genuine interest. "This man is not only a brilliant scientist, but a spiritually advanced human being."

He gave me the contact information for Dr. Paul Wendland,

who lives in Southern California. I decided that I would fly to Los Angeles to meet with Dr. Wendland if he was willing to see me. I burst through the double doors of the Opera House out into the sunlight, struck by the stunning beauty of the day and the majesty of the mountains that cradled the Sun Valley Lodge.

Dr. Wendland agreed to meet with me, and he was even kind enough to invite me to his home. I promptly flew there with my recording device and list of questions in hand. I later visited Dr. Wendland a second time with Jim. We met Dr. Wendland's wife and daughter, both of whom are delightful. When he initially opened the door to invite me in, I was immediately taken by his size and warm demeanor. For some reason, I flashed to Baloo the bear in the Disney film *The Jungle Book* from Tanner's childhood days. I think it was his easy smile, his generous spirit, and his larger-than-life presence that prompted the comparison.

With broad shoulders and big hands, he towered over me, stepping aside so I could sit with him in his cozy kitchen. He lived in Ventura near the ocean, and the sunlight was casting brilliant rays through the curtains as we sat down to coffee and Danish. I felt comfortable and relaxed in his presence. He was contemplative, and he spoke softly. My original perception of Dr. Wendland physically like Baloo was quickly melting. This was not just a warm and friendly man; this was a wise and thoughtful man with a unique tenderness and gentleness.

Asking his permission to record our session, I began our discussion.

"As I indicated on the phone, I'm trying to come to terms with some strange events that I've experienced since my husband died. I am hoping you can help me. I'm not sure exactly where to begin, but before we get started on my story, I was hoping you would share yours with me," I said.

Paul Wendland is an experimental physicist with a Ph.D. from UCLA. He has undergone a personal transformation as a result of his inquiries into spirituality after a stellar career in physics—and I literally mean stellar. His company built the starlight navigation sensors for the *Voyager* spacecraft. In other words, I was having the first conversation of my life with a genuine rocket scientist.

And unlike some people I've known who think they are rocket scientists, Dr. Wendland is actually quite modest. "Measuring light and understanding light has been my pursuit my whole life," he told me. "I have concluded I don't understand it. I've also studied quantum physics my whole life. I don't understand that either."

Dr. Wendland's doctoral dissertation was on electro absorption in silicon. (I have no idea what that is.) He taught physics in UCLA's engineering department for two years before leaving the academic world and launching his own company, United Detector Technology, which built the *Voyager* sensors. He was successful in the business world, founding or cofounding several companies, the last of which was sold to 3M.

He grew up in a family of fundamentalist Lutherans, content with the knowledge that there was both a heaven and a hell and that he was destined for heaven since he'd been "saved." But at twelve or thirteen years of age, he began to question that view. He took physics in high school and found it fascinating and easy. As he studied at UCLA, he began to see life as quarks and electrons that formed DNA, which then formed humans. The notion of God no longer seemed necessary, he told me. He said he was a fan of Algernon Charles Swinburne's poem that described death as eternal sleep, a cessation of all sounds and sights. It struck him as peaceful.

The seeds of yet another change in his spiritual views were planted by his roommate at UCLA, who had a question for this atheist: "You've got life and death figured out. What about love?"

Love didn't fit quite so neatly into his view. But Dr. Wendland continued on his path. "I was focused on making money and was happy in my atheism."

Much later, after he sold his second company and was "footloose and fancy-free," he began to meditate and do his own reading about spirituality. His question was, "What is the essence of consciousness?"

This is good, I thought. If I could begin to understand the essence of consciousness, as he put it, then maybe I could begin to understand if this essence had the ability to exist beyond the realm of our human lives. And this could be a window into the appearance of the handprint.

"As I explored consciousness," Dr. Wendland said, "I came to believe that questioning the validity of science or the truth of religion was simply missing the point. We should be asking ourselves the question, 'Is there *more* than this physical reality which we all inhabit?' I was drawn to a new path, a mystical journey exploring nonphysical realities."

Nonphysical realities were exactly what I had come to learn about. I found his life story fascinating. Here was this brilliant man in his early seventies who had grappled with the same questions I was now addressing as a novice. And he had come from a fact-based background as a scientist, just as I had come from the black-and-white (no pun intended) world of newspapers. He was curious about whether there was more than the physical realm in life, and he wanted to understand exactly what consciousness meant. I was captivated by his story.

During a spiritual study group, he was introduced to a book by Robert Monroe called *Journeys Out of the Body* and attended a seminar at the Monroe Institute in Faber, Virginia. The course was life changing for him in several ways. Dr. Wendland experienced having lived previous lives, and he met Shelley, who is now his wife (and was his wife in a previous life, he says). He went on to have many out-of-body experiences and visits to multiple past lives. He is convinced from these personal experiences that there is "more."

I was learning that this man had been on an expedition for much of his life. He wasn't content to just go with the flow of everyday life. He didn't profess to have all the answers. Quite the opposite. He was more interested in formulating the right questions. His scientific background made him naturally curious. But where he might diverge from other scientists was in his passion to go beyond the study of physical properties. And he was genuinely spiritual, as well.

"The spiritual tradition that fits me best now is Christianity, and I have a deep and abiding connection to Christ," he said. He also believes that many valid spiritual paths lead to the "all that is."

We related to each other as Christians and as two people who believe in the spirit world. Where we diverged was in his capacity as a physicist, not to mention his sheer brainpower. I wanted to explore his perspective, as a scientist, on what I had been experiencing.

"How would a scientist react to the handprint I saw?" I asked.

"The view of the majority of scientists is that everything in reality is physically based, just electrons and quarks and their cousins—there is no 'more,'" he said. "In other words, even our consciousness reduces to these elements. No aspect of consciousness exists separately from brain function. When brain function ceases, you cease to exist. That's the traditional thinking.

"But if we're just a bunch of neurons and there is not more," Dr. Wendland pointed out, "then how is it we possess free will, a quality that makes humans unique as a species? Our deliberate and individual choices mean we operate on more than instinct and hardwired reactions to the environment. The free will we exercise in life allows us to learn, which is what makes the human condition so meaningful."

And then it hit me that it was possible that I was supposed to be struggling with the meaning of these events because, as Dr. Wendland pointed out, it's the only way learning takes place. Jim often became frustrated and asked why the communications from the other side were so difficult to decipher. I understood his frustrations. I wanted an easily digestible answer too. I asked Dr. Wendland the question Jim and I had been mulling over for a while.

"If the spirit world or Max is trying to tell me something, why don't they communicate in a fashion that we can more easily understand and interpret? If they want our help, why aren't they more helpful?" I asked.

Dr. Wendland responded, "A reason those in another reality don't communicate fully with us is that crossing over into our world requires great effort. But more important, if the spirits shared all the information they have, and we, as a result, knew all the consequences of our actions in this life before we took them, we would be deprived of the opportunity to grow from discovering those outcomes ourselves," he said. "If we knew all, we couldn't learn. And the point of each life is to learn and experience different attributes of what it means to be human. We are part of the learning of the whole universe. Each of our experiences contributes to the whole, so we need those experiences to be completely freely made."

I took this to mean that without free will and the ability to learn, we would merely be existing. *Oh, what a disaster that would be,* I thought. I cannot imagine life without personal freedom, without the ability to exercise our own individual choices based on our own judgment. A prescription would negate choice, and without choice, where is the satisfaction in life?

I was anxious to share all of this with Jim. He had a very interesting reaction. "I define free will as the ability to act at one's own discretion without prior determination or divine [spiritual] intervention," he said. "Without free will in our lives we are merely performing a role in a play. The play has been written, we've seen all the acts up to this point, and we are moving inexorably to its end. Without free will in life, what's the point of living? Clearly the actors aren't as engaged when they have no impact on the end of the play. In fact, you could make a strong case that even the playwright would find it boring."

And so Jim and I were aligned in believing in free will and the power it holds. This also means I have to accept not having all the answers. The mysteries I am seeking to solve may not be solvable. Perhaps I'll simply need to do a better job of learning to live with ambiguity.

I asked Dr. Wendland to elaborate on his personal view of consciousness.

"Our consciousness is separate from the brain. It is our essence—our soul. At the lower levels, consciousness has form—our body—but as we move up, there is less interest in form and more in thought. At the highest level, however, there is no form—only light."

Further, Dr. Wendland said he believes that consciousness is the foundation of everything and brings the physical into reality at all moments of time. But he is a realist; he knows it will take time to prove this scientifically. He continued with a hypothesis about how we as people play an active role in affecting our outcomes through our consciousness.

"Since consciousness is more than physical matter, each individual has an ability to affect outcome," he said. "One might say there is a force from the physical brain to outside matter, but I believe the effect is more subtle than this. The understanding of the mechanism of consciousness interacting with the physical world will constitute the main line of scientific breakthrough in the next few hundred years and will lead to a more complete understanding of ourselves. At present we do not have such a theory or enough experimental data to form this theory."

He continued, "Experiment is the cornerstone of all physical-world study. It is the true basis of science. I honor this outlook in my own physics studies. Theory is useful as a unifying factor, but experiment is the true basis of science."

Addressing the hypothesis that we as humans can affect outcome, Dr. Wendland recently worked with Dr. Dean Radin, senior scientist at the Institute of Noetic Sciences, which is devoted to the study of consciousness. Dr. Wendland and Dr. Radin conducted an experiment, and the results were published in an article in *Physics Essays* titled "Consciousness and the Double-Slit Interference Pattern."

It's a complicated article, not intended for laypersons (like me). But, in essence, it is a study of psychokinesis, the ability of the mind to affect matter. The question Dr. Wendland and

Dr. Radin addressed was whether deep meditation and intention could affect the behavior of light as it passes through two slits. The experiment proposed that consciousness collapses the quantum wave function of light in a predictable way. The results showed that it did to a small—but significant—degree.

The experiment itself was based on a simple concept. Two small slits are made very close together in a piece of metal. When you shine a light through these slits, you would expect to get one pattern, Dr. Wendland explained. In fact, you get two patterns of light and dark regions that go on into infinity in both directions. "This is a quintessential quantum experiment," he said.

Dr. Wendland and Dr. Radin wanted to test whether the conscious intent of a person could make the light pattern change. If a person wanted the light to go through one slit instead of both, would the resulting light pattern change?

Guess what? It did. The effect was very small, detectable only with modern high-powered equipment, he said. "It's probably a good thing that the effect is minor and that people have varying ability to affect matter," he added. "If we had large psychokinesis, the result would be chaotic."

This idea that human observation can change physical reality is not new. I learned from Dr. Wendland that it's actually embedded in a theory called the Copenhagen interpretation. He explained that this theory was formulated in 1924 by Niels Bohr and Werner Heisenberg, two of the founders of quantum physics. What they found "made them pull their hair out," he said.

I didn't want to keep interrupting Dr. Wendland and asking him to stop and explain everything, given the gap between his scientific knowledge and mine. What I did instead was quickly scratch a note on my pad: "go back—do homework—quantum physics." This is a little like saying "go to Himalayas—climb Mt. Everest—29,000 feet above sea level."

Later, as I sat at home one night in the evening, reading up on quantum physics, my mind began to wander. (Whose wouldn't?) I realized I actually remembered learning about photons (light particles) forty years earlier. I was in science class. It was 1969, my senior year at Taft High School in Hamilton, Ohio. On the day we studied subatomic particles (protons, neutrons, and electrons), the problem I was having was that I was sitting on a high wooden stool next to a lab counter, like all the students, so I had trouble listening because my feet were dangling without any support. This, in turn, made me focus on my shoes, which then led me to wonder whether I needed new ones, which led me to think about how soon I could go shopping. And since I wasn't exactly able to understand every single thing our teacher was saying anyway, when I did look up at the chalkboard (no PowerPoint presentations in those days), I mainly concentrated on not falling off the stool. But now that I was in my late fifties, I obviously had matured and advanced. Right?

But I digress. What I eventually discovered in my own research is that quantum physics is a branch of physics that addresses the behavior of energy and matter on an extremely small scale. This area of physics is governed by a different set of rules than traditional physics. For instance, quantum physicists hold that the location of very small particles is only determined when they are observed. Therefore, perhaps we can actually influence them if we have intention, as the experiment of Dr. Radin and Dr. Wendland suggests.

What is surprising about the Copenhagen interpretation is that under this theory, there is no description of physical reality. "Rather, there are only probabilities of observing or measuring something. Only when something is actually observed does it move from an indeterminate state to an actual state," Dr. Wendland explained. "So I take this to mean that conscious observation is required to bring anything and everything into existence."

If I understood this, I thought, nothing exists physically until we observe it. A tantalizing concept. I was intrigued. Does this mean the handprint wasn't there until I observed it? Did I somehow have an unconscious intention to create the powdery image? Or is it possible that Max put the handprint on the mirror with his strong intention, an intention that traveled from one dimension to another?

I was curious about something else. I asked Dr. Wendland, "If the Copenhagen interpretation is correct, then how did anything exist in the early universe before we were around to observe things?"

His playful but insightful response was a limerick:

There once was a man who said, God
Must think it exceedingly odd
If he finds that this tree
Continues to be
When there's no one about in the quad.

And the reply:

Dear sir, your astonishment's odd.
I am always about in the quad.
And that's why the tree
Will continue to be
Since observed by, yours faithfully, God.

"In other words, God is the ever-present and infinite consciousness, the observer and creator of all that exists. If we are in God's image, our souls must also have a consciousness that observes and creates reality."

I asked Dr. Wendland how his learning and experiences have affected him.

"It's made me realize that what you have doesn't count," he said. "It's what you do for others that matters. In fact, that is how you build spiritual power—by giving it away. The more you give, the more you receive. If you project fear, you get fear back. If you project love, you get love back."

Now we were discussing something I didn't have to research: love. My idea of the power of love had blossomed over the course of my life. But it wasn't until I lost Max that I was confronted with the full magnitude of what love means. Max is teaching me that love transcends this world and the next. And even though the physical part of life is no longer attainable with him, the love remains a constant in my heart. I believe he carried this same love in his heart with him to the other side, to heaven or to whatever nonphysical plane in which he now exists. And I believe it's this love that powered his ability to reach across from the spirit world to this world.

Dr. Wendland reinforced what I was experiencing. His "altered states and nonphysical planes" taught him that there is more than physical existence and that humans have just begun to explore and understand these additional realities.

"We are at the very earliest beginnings of the quest for knowledge and understanding," he told me, "not, as many leading scientists propose, near the end."

CHAPTER 11

Can We Travel Outside Our Bodies?

When we meet someone and end up falling in love at an older age, say, late fifties or early sixties, the baggage we stow in our memory banks is not the size of the Dopp kit we toted in our twenties. Now we're wielding a suitcase with the heft of a steamer trunk. It's quite possible that within that trunk, there are some things stashed snugly in cubbyholes. I was carting around one of those memories about a dream I'd had shortly after Max died. And now it was surfacing in my mind, probably because I was reminiscing about the vision of Dad visiting my bedside after he had died in February 2007. I was eager to share my older dream with Jim, and true to form, he listened and was open.

One night about two to three weeks after Max died, I followed my regular pattern of going to bed around ten p.m. I often read for at least a half hour before falling asleep. Over the years I developed a consistent sleeping habit of eight hours a night, but since Max's death, those dependable hours had been fractured, particularly early on. I would often wake up in the night, turn to Max's side of the bed, and instinctively reach out for him. I had that warm-milky sliver of a moment when I could actually believe he was alive. Then I would touch the cold, empty sheet, and the stark reminder that he was gone would hit. I was continually unnerved by this. Repetition didn't seem to teach me anything. The routine made sleep problematic.

On this particular night something remarkable interrupted the routine. I can only describe the experience as a dream or dreamlike state of being. In the middle of the night, I awoke to find myself traveling down the hallway from my bedroom to the front of the house. Traveling, not walking. I was floating or flying horizontally, presumably unattached from my body. This was obviously impossible. But for reasons I don't fully comprehend, it seemed normal, even exhilarating. I had a sense of flying parallel and relatively close to the ceiling without bumping into it. I could see straight down to the floor. I felt light and airy, slowly gliding through the air like a boat in smooth waters. I noticed that the walls were the exact ones in our home, warm wheat yellow with white crown molding and covered with our family photos. I saw our large antique pine apothecary flush against the wall and our Persian rug on the hardwood floor.

Nothing was distorted the way it is normally in a dream. Everything was in order, except, of course, for the fact that I was floating in midair. I felt like Mary Martin in *Peter Pan*, minus the tunic and tights. But unlike Peter Pan, I was not so sure of myself. As I navigated down our hallway, I came to a corner and turned left heading toward the kitchen and living room. I looked to the right toward our library and glanced at our books on the bookshelves. Looking through the large bay window to the outdoors, I saw the neighbors' front porch light across the street, casting a soft golden ray onto the grass. Just as the hallway was our actual hallway, these rooms and the front porch of our neighbors' home were as they always were.

As I turned my eyes from the library back toward the living room and kitchen, I saw Max. Yes, it was Max, without question, and in all the fullness of his healthy self, wearing a gray sweater, olive cords, and brown loafers; his silver hair was neatly combed. The outline of his muscular frame was just as it had been before he got sick. He was standing next to the refrigerator and the small kitchen desk we used for notes and grocery lists. His back was to me.

I couldn't believe it! I said to myself, *I must have been wrong about Max dying, because here he is! He isn't gone after all. He has been alive all this time.*

With that thought, I reached out, extending my hand to touch him on the right shoulder. But instead of coming to rest on a strong muscle, my hand passed straight through him and out the other side. The body I perceived as solid was a vapor. He never turned around. I never saw his face. Then he disappeared altogether, fading into thin air. Just like that, he was gone.

Stunned and shaken, I came to my senses and told myself that of course he could not have been standing there in person. Max had died on May 8.

So what had just happened? Had I seen his spirit? Was it a ghost? Had I imagined the whole thing? And aside from the apparition, let's not forget that I was hovering in midair. I am only too aware of how strange this all sounds. Maybe it was just a dream. But I don't believe it was a dream in the classic sense, because it was too exact, particularly the physical parts of our home. There was a precision to the trip I took down the hallway and into the other rooms. No distortions, no sidetracks.

Whatever it was, there is no doubt that the impetus was my grief. I was open in a way I had never been before. And now, sharing it with Jim and watching his nonjudgmental response gave me the confidence and the willpower to take the next step.

I decided to research out-of-body experiences and what it might mean to be in an altered state of consciousness. I remembered what Dr. Wendland had shared with me. The phrase was popularized more than thirty years ago in a book by Robert Monroe. Monroe was a radio broadcast entrepreneur who tested the boundaries of consciousness on himself. Monroe's legacy, the Monroe Institute (TMI), performs research on consciousness and has developed a retreat where visitors can learn to use techniques to bring their conscious awareness to different levels. In this deep state between meditation and sleep, visitors experience other states, sometimes including past lives, as Dr. Paul Wendland had discussed.

I thought it would be helpful to visit the Monroe Institute as a part of my journey, hoping to learn what I could about this dreamlike state of altered consciousness. Would I be able to find validation that consciousness exists outside the body? I asked Jim to go with me. Together we traveled to TMI in the foothills of the Blue Ridge Mountains to meet with Dr. Carol de la Herran, the executive director and president of TMI, who was kind enough to arrange a tour of the facilities for us.

The campus is serene and beautiful, with meditation areas, a scenic creek, and walking trails that wind through a forest. At night you can see panoramic views of the mountains and stars from the roof deck. We toured the two TMI facilities, which extend over several hundred acres. After the tour, Dr. de la Herran, who held Ph.D.s in psychology and energy medicine, a law degree, and an MBA in international marketing, greeted us, and we talked in her office.

Dr. de la Herran explained to me that Mr. Monroe's fascination with consciousness began when he learned about Russian experiments to accelerate the gathering of knowledge through what was called "sleep learning." During the cold war years, he began to look into the idea himself. And since he was familiar with audio production methods from the radio industry, he figured he was his own perfect test case. This reminded me of Stephen Barr, who used himself for testing the biofeedback mechanisms he was designing in his first job, a choice that led to a new career. So, too, with Robert Monroe.

In 1958, while experimenting with sleep learning, he began to record sensations accompanied by a bright light. Six weeks later he had his first out-of-body experience.

He felt himself floating to the top of his bedroom and bumping into the ceiling. It was exactly the same thing that happened to me, except I didn't bump into the ceiling. He didn't know what was happening to him. Was it his spirit or soul? And who was that man (him) in bed with his wife? He clawed his way back down to the bed and into his body. He consulted with some doctors and psychiatrists, and they found nothing wrong with him. Unlike me and my one experience, this happened to Mr. Monroe repeatedly, naturally leading him to a desire to understand it. So he documented his experiences.

As his company and research evolved, he founded the Monroe Institute. He died in 1995, but specialists in psychology, biochemistry, psychiatry, electrical engineering, and physics have continued to help with TMI's work. Today, TMI is a nonprofit research and educational organization dedicated to enhancing the understanding of human consciousness and whether we can exist separately from our bodies.

I asked Dr. de la Herran to talk about Robert Monroe, whom she knew personally. "Bob," she said, "was not a particularly religious person, and he never wanted to be seen as a guru. He didn't want to tell people what they should believe. He was interested in using science to create tools that could help others discover their own truths. The only dogma we have around here is that when guests arrive, we ask them to consider that they might be more than their physical body, at least while they are here."

During Mr. Monroe's experiments on himself, "being the businessman that he was, he kept copious notes," Dr. de la Herran said.

He was initially reluctant to publish a book, she said. He told her, "Absolutely not—that's my private life. What would my colleagues in radio think of me if they read such a book? They'll think I'm nuts." (I can relate to this response.) On further reflection, however, it occurred to him that his colleagues in radio were highly unlikely to read such a book anyway, so why not?

"Bob fell into his first book, the one that got all this started, by accident. Dr. Charles Tart played a pivotal role," she told us. Dr. Tart, a researcher for more than fifty years, is a legend in the field of parapsychology. When I later contacted him, he told me the story.

"In the fall of 1965, my family moved to Charlottesville, as I had taken a job as an instructor in the psychiatry department at the University of Virginia medical school there, with time to do some ESP research," Dr. Tart told me. "My wife and I got to know Bob Monroe almost immediately through mutual friends.

Bob gave me a copy of the complete manuscript of *Journeys Out of the Body*. I read it and was quite excited. When I asked him about publication plans, he told me he had sent it to his agent in New York City about a year ago and had not heard a response in all that time. This made me think his agent was freaked-out by the material and hadn't actually done anything toward finding a publisher."

So Dr. Tart sent a copy of the manuscript to the late Bill Whitehead, an editor at Doubleday, which had published the paperback edition of Dr. Tart's *Altered States of Consciousness*. Mr. Whitehead took the manuscript home after work because Dr. Tart had recommended it. The editor started reading it late in the evening and "became so fascinated he could not put it down and go to bed," Dr. Tart said. "Doubleday thus became the publisher for Bob's book."

Despite his belief that none of his radio colleagues would ever see the book, one week after the release of *Journeys Out of the Body*, Mr. Monroe was on a yacht with the president of NBC Radio when the president's wife came out of the cabin holding the book and asked Mr. Monroe to sign it. "She's a psychic," her husband told Monroe.

So much for anonymity.

Mr. Monroe firmly believed that consciousness is more than the brain. The techniques Mr. Monroe developed to help people reach other states of consciousness resulted from the same openness that has helped many scientists see broader implications for their experimental data or theories. During our tour of TMI, we had seen small rooms with headphones, known as CHEC (controlled holistic environmental chamber) units, which are "semi-isolation chambers," Dr. de la Herran explained.

Mr. Monroe didn't invent the technology that forms the

foundation of these headphone and booth tools. We learned that the technology was discovered in 1865 and was first used to test hearing. It's based on what happens when someone hears two different sounds at the same time, one in each ear. The brain works to make the two sounds identical by creating sound waves that are equal to the difference between the two sounds. For example, if someone has a sound of 100 cycles per second in one ear and a sound of 104 cycles per second in the other ear, the brain will create waves of 4 cycles per second, which is right at the edge between theta and delta brain waves. (Theta waves are meditative or creative, and delta waves are what we experience in our deep sleep.) Mr. Monroe described his discovery of this "edge" state as "a window to consciousness."

The technology that Mr. Monroe devised has up to thirty-five layers of sound coming through the headphones, allowing the hemispheres of the brain to move into synchronized patterns.

"With the analytic and the intuitive sides working together, you achieve an optimal state of brain functioning. The combinations of sound help get you to an altered state, and it helps keep you there. Bob gave these altered states numbers. Focus 12, for example, is a focus for intuition and guidance," Dr. de la Herran explained.

"Does this mean you are stuck wearing headphones to enjoy the benefits of the technology?" I asked.

"No, because you can learn to do it on your own, usually within a weeklong program, as the brain creates new neural pathways," Dr. de la Herran said. TMI trainers think of the headphones as training wheels, she said.

What happens in these sessions can vary. Sometimes participants move to a state of no time. Another program is dedicated to moving in time. You can go back to the early part of your life, or even past lives, to move beyond beliefs or emotions that have limited your progress in life. You can assess your current situation and gain perspective. And you can go forward in time to see your potential future and help you navigate to your highest purpose.

I asked how Mr. Monroe's philosophy would be carried on, and Dr. de la Herran's answer was that he didn't have a philosophy. He did believe that what we call spirit has many manifestations, she said. "Interestingly, he never used the word 'reincarnation' because he felt it implied one life is after the other. He believed that in other realms, time doesn't exist," she said.

She ended by saying that Robert Monroe's primary message was to explore. "He always taught us to go find our own answers." This has resonated with me, especially since Dr. de la Herran passed away in July 2013 after a short illness. I am honored to include some insight into her work here.

My dream about an out-of-body experience was astonishing, and for me one of a kind. But it wasn't the last time I had a startling dream involving Max. On another occasion, around six months after Max died, I was asleep in the bed of our master bedroom in Napa and awoke in the middle of the night sensing I was not alone. As I glanced to the left, I saw a vision of Max standing next to the bed. He was perfectly still and just staring down at me. I could see he was strong and robust, filling out his clothes with the full weight of his two-hundred-pound body before he was diagnosed with cancer. Our eyes locked and stayed connected for an indeterminate time, almost as if there was no time. No words passed his lips. Everything I felt he was communicating, just as it had been in the dream with my dad, was sensed, not heard. The message I received was that Max loved me and was no longer suffering. If he had been speaking with a bullhorn, it would not have been clearer.

The time we spent connected was intimate and brought us together once again. What I remember happening next was a gradual fading of light from his eyes. It was the same light I saw him lose when he died. His soul seemed to recede until finally I observed only his body. It stood before me without him inside of it. At least that's how it felt in the dream. His true essence was gone. And then shortly after, the vision of his physical self faded, evaporating into nothingness.

It left me with a strange emotional amalgam of comfort and sadness.

CHAPTER 12

Ghosts: Real or Imagined?

Were the dreams I had, like most dreams, a function of my own imagination? Or had I been visited from the spirit world by Max and my dad? If they did pay me a visit, does that mean they were ghosts when they came? Or were they spirits? What's the difference between the two?

Slightly embarrassed (yet again), I wanted to see if Jim would join me to investigate ghosts. Everything was out in the open now about having seen Max and my dad, and Jim was intrigued. But going the next step of actually researching ghosts could be pushing it, I thought. I decided to tread lightly. I figured there might be a limit to just how idiosyncratic I could be and still be credible in his eyes. Plus, I knew Jim was far more interested in the scientific realm than the ethereal when it came to research.

I decided to employ a tactic that a psychologist friend had taught me years earlier. He said if you want to engage in a conversation that might be difficult, do it on a walk, a bicycle ride, or a trip in the car. Instead of sitting across the table staring into each other's eyes, facing the same direction is less intimate and consequently less intimidating if you have an awkward subject to tackle. So I suggested to Jim that we take a walk. We talked about plans for the weekend and errands that needed to be done, and when I felt the conversation had reached a crescendo of mundaneness, I jumped in with my question.

"Have you ever had any situation where you were confronted by a ghost? As a child or an adult?" I asked, mustering the most nonchalant voice in the history of humankind.

Looking over at me with a slightly quizzical expression, Jim responded in a matter-of-fact tone with just two words: "No. Never." Then he leaned down to tie his shoelace, seemingly happy to be distracted from the ghost question.

"Never...ever? What about when your dad died?" I said.

"No. Nothing. Sorry," he replied, conveying a tone that was almost apologetic, as if he wanted to say yes, but couldn't, because it wasn't true. Meanwhile, I was thinking how far Jim had stretched to accommodate all the events I had experienced. The last thing I wanted to do was push too hard and lose the credibility I had maintained with him. So I dropped the subject.

Yet I couldn't stop wondering why most people (including me) spend most of their lives being afraid of ghosts. Is it because of the spooky tales we heard as children? When I was a kid, we used to tell goofy ghost stories around campfires. We'd plop down cross-legged on the ground, our arms circling our knees as the embers from the fire popped and shot out into the woods. We would sit for hours telling stories while the adults stoked the fire and sat on canvas chairs one row behind us. I especially remember my two older brothers, Kurt and Brian, ganging up with my cousins to try to scare the girls. Mainly they'd jump out from behind a big oak tree and yell "Oooohhh" a bunch.

As an adult, I'd never thought about ghosts. It wasn't until Max and Dad died and appeared in my dreams that I had an interest. Eventually this curiosity led me to Loyd Auerbach.

Loyd, who wittily calls himself the "ghost guy," is an expert in his field of phantoms. I first met him at an annual meeting of Forever Family Foundation, a group dedicated to helping bereaved people and supporting scientific study of the afterlife. Loyd, who had just been elected president of the foundation, spoke on a panel. He got my attention when he cited a quote from science-fiction author Kathleen Sky: "There is no such thing as supernatural—there are only things we don't understand yet."

Apparently Jim's only exposure to ghosts was the *Casper the Friendly Ghost* animated cartoon show on TV when he was a young boy. So I thought he might be interested in joining me when Loyd invited me to visit his home in Northern California. Loyd could not have been nicer, more open, or friendlier. He took the edge off any apprehension we had on the topic. We knew Loyd was a good teacher because we had seen his delivery at the conference. What made him so engaging as a speaker were his personality and his natural way of using humor and personal stories to illustrate his points. He's the same in private. He peers sharply through his glasses with a twinkle in his eye. And his easy use of self-deprecating humor shows he has his ego firmly in check and doesn't take himself too seriously, as if he's *the* authority.

As a bonus, his hobby is making chocolate, so we left with a small bag of chocolate, the contents of which we quickly devoured. As I unpeeled the shiny foil wrapper, I was pleasantly surprised to see a tiny embossed bunch of little spooks, reminiscent of the Casper cartoon. No doubt that resonated with Jim.

Loyd graduated from Northwestern University with a bachelor's degree in cultural anthropology and from John F. Kennedy University with a master's degree in parapsychology. He is on the faculty of Atlantic University in Virginia Beach, Virginia, and is the creator and principal instructor of the Parapsychological Studies Certificate Program at HCH Institute in Lafayette, California. He is the author of eight books on parapsychology. His most recent is *The Ghost Detectives' Guide to Haunted San Francisco*.

Loyd has appeared on *The View, Larry King Live, The Oprah Winfrey Show*, and *Late Night with David Letterman*. He has participated in paranormal-related programs for the Travel Channel, the Learning Channel, A&E, the Biography Channel, the History Channel, and the Discovery Channel. He is also a professional mentalist and psychic entertainer and former magician.

I asked Loyd how he got interested in this subject. "I wish I had an impressive answer," he said, "but it was actually watching television shows as a kid, such as *Topper, The Twilight Zone*, and *One Step Beyond*. I also read a lot of mythology, science fiction, and especially superhero comic books. I was a science geek. I just had to get into this field."

I got straight to an essential question for me. "Since we hear the term all the time, what is a ghost?"

Loyd answered, "While the word 'ghost' covers a variety of experiences in different cultures, most people use the term to mean a spirit or some form of a person after they have died, but typically the general public uses the term for any figure seen or heard, whether a conscious spirit or a haunting. These are, in fact, two different things."

I asked him to explain the difference between a conscious spirit and a haunting.

"A conscious spirit is an apparition," Loyd said. "It is the consciousness of a human surviving death of the body. It is capable of interacting with the living."

So this must have been what I saw with Max and my dad. Loyd said the living person perceives an apparition by seeing, hearing, feeling, or smelling the spirit. In my case, with Max and Dad, I only saw them. Apparitions tend to stay in places where they had some psychological or emotional connection or relationship during their lifetime, he said. This certainly applied to Max. "But they can appear in other places too," he said, which would explain Dad's visit.

Hauntings are in a different category. Hauntings involve ghostly figures or voices that are location-specific and not able to interact with us, Loyd said. They are like videos of something that has occurred in that place and been imprinted into the environment. These hauntings are not conscious spirits.

The figures witnessed in hauntings tend to be repetitive, both in what's experienced by the living person and in when they occur. People report seeing, hearing, feeling, or smelling a presence that's typically engaged in some sort of activity. It could be a man's figure walking up and down the hallway or footsteps heard from the attic. Speaking or interacting with these spirits is futile because they just continue to go about their business as though you're not even there. In other words, they are essentially holograms instead of conscious beings capable of interacting, Loyd said.

We talked a bit more about my dreams and how I had seen Max the first time about three weeks after he died and had seen Dad about a month after he died. I learned that this was not the norm.

"Most, but certainly not all, apparitions typically occur within forty-eight to seventy-two hours of the person's death, as if the person is coming to say good-bye and is seeking interaction and closure," Loyd said. "Longer-term apparitions tend to have a psychological or emotional need to stay here. Such needs include denial of death, fear of what's next, unfinished business, a strong desire to stay with one's loved one, or even frustration at a life cut short."

With Max, all of these reasons could apply. With Dad, not so. I think he was saying good-bye.

Jim jumped in and asked whether anyone had documented proof of apparitions using technology of any kind. Lloyd's answer was unfortunately no.

"In my field, we define apparitions as a form of consciousness," he said, "but mainstream science is still up in the air on a universal definition of consciousness itself. In other words, there's no physical evidence for consciousness per se among the living other than our own behavior and thoughts. If we can't prove the existence of consciousness in the brain, where we assume it is, how can we prove the existence of consciousness outside the body?"

According to Loyd, the only way to study consciousness, whether it is consciousness of the living or consciousness of the dead, is by the experiences of people. His area of study is parapsychology, which is primarily a social science. And though measuring tools used in the physical sciences are included, the best evidence comes from people, or witnesses. And the strongest cases are those in which there are multiple witnesses and information provided by the experiencer that can later be verified.

Bottom line: as long as the issue of consciousness is still up in the air, so is proof of ghosts.

I asked Loyd whether he has ever seen or felt spirits himself.

"Over the years I've learned to pay more attention to my own perceptions," he said. "I have not seen an apparition, but I have felt, smelled, and sensed them, even having one repeatedly walk through me. Just a few years ago, I had my first auditory experience."

Then he told me a great story. It was about Loyd's good friend Martin Caidin, a science-fiction writer and creator of the television series *The Six Million Dollar Man*, which emanated from his novel *Cyborg*. Mr. Caidin was a larger-than-life character and a big cigar smoker. Just before he died, he told Loyd, "I'm going to come back and haunt you, Auerbach."

Mr. Caidin knew a lot of people in the aviation world, was an unofficial consultant to NASA, and even knew aerospace engineer Wernher Von Braun back when the space program was in its infancy. When Mr. Caidin died, Loyd really expected him to show up.

"I had agreed to drink a couple of shots of rum in his honor," Loyd said. "I still didn't see him. But a little over a week went by, and I was driving to the airport at seven a.m. to fly to Portland for a meeting. My car at the time was three months old and still had that new-car smell.

"No one had smoked in my car.

"All of a sudden my car fills up with the smell of cigar smoke. I knew it was him. It lasted until seven or eight minutes after seven a.m. As soon as I got to Portland, I called a friend of mine in New Jersey who also knew Marty. I said, 'Bob, you're not going to believe what just happened to me.'

"He interrupted me and said, 'Loyd, you must be psychic.'

"'Yes, I am,' I joked. 'Bob, why do you think I am?'"

"He said, 'I was out flying my Cessna to New Jersey, and about ten minutes after ten a.m. my cockpit fills with the smell of cigar smoke.'"

"Knowing he was three hours ahead of me, on eastern time, I got a little excited but merely said, 'Oh, really.'"

"'But that's not the best part,' he told me. 'A friend of mine and Caidin's was flying his plane in Florida at the same time, and his cockpit filled up with cigar smoke, too.'"

"Later, after we checked with all our mutual friends, twenty-five people, including us, either had their car or plane fill with cigar smoke in succession before and after the same time. So that's my experience. But everyone has some degree of psychic sensitivity. Unfortunately we are educated out of it as we grow up. Everyone can develop it to some extent, but it's not so much developing as noticing what's going on."

And if I've learned anything on my journey, I've learned to pay attention and notice what's going on. Loyd is so right about that.

CHAPTER 13

Magic Carpets

In the late fall of 2008 I had another encounter with the golden threads. It took place in the living room of our Sun Valley home. I was talking on the phone with Tanner when I noticed over in the far corner three or four horizontal golden threads about eighteen inches long. They were floating just above the large globe I had given Jim for his birthday. Just as in the two previous cases, they looked like corn silk or a web, golden in color and not connected to anything.

But this time when I touched one, it didn't disappear. Instead, a small rectangle formed behind my finger, like a jewel on a necklace. The threads lasted about five minutes and then disappeared. I don't know why it took me so long to think of researching these phenomena of golden threads. What I learned from my reading was fascinating.

I believe I was seeing examples of Indra's Net, also called Indra's Jewels or Indra's Pearls, named after a story from ancient Vedic texts about a net that the god Indra cast over his palace.

It's a metaphor used to illustrate the Buddhist concept of interpenetration, which means everything in the universe is related to everything else. Each "jewel" in the net reflects into infinity all the other mutual relationships, much as two facing mirrors will reflect an image into infinity. A change in one jewel means a change, however small, in every other jewel in the net.

None of the pictures I found on the Internet or in books looked exactly like what I had seen, but there was a strong resemblance. I also learned that quantum physics has a concept that very nearly matches the ancient net metaphor. This quantum concept, called Bell's Theorem, is complicated. But in simple terms, Bell's Theorem says that our world is nonlocal, meaning things can be connected across time and space. And it's not just that they are connected. They can act as one. I wonder, does this include people?

In early November Jim and I drove from Sun Valley to our Yountville home. We had plans to visit friends and spend Thanksgiving with Tanner, who would be on break from UCLA. On Wednesday afternoon, November 5, we arrived, unpacked, and settled in for a monthlong stay in our cozy retreat among the redwoods and vineyards. We took a long walk in the neighborhood and then enjoyed a fabulous meal at Bouchon, our favorite local restaurant.

On Thursday morning we awoke to a surprise. As we walked around the corner hallway leading from our bedroom to the kitchen, we noticed that the Karastan rug, a five-by-eight-foot rug that I had brought from our kitchen in Sacramento and was usually centered evenly in the middle of the kitchen floor, had moved off center by about six inches.

By now we were veterans of the moving-rug phenomenon, but we were still skeptical. Maybe we had misjudged where the rug was the day before. So this time we used a little more discipline.

Beginning Thursday morning we positioned the rug flush against the left wall at the base of the molding coming into the kitchen. By Saturday morning it ended up about nine inches from where it began. It eventually butted up against the cabinets on the other side of the room. Yes, this heavy rug with a mat under it had propelled itself almost a foot from left to right. Preposterous.

We surveyed our household inventory of sophisticated scientific instruments and came up with an index card and a tape measure. I know the scientists I interviewed for this book are groaning right now. It's not lost on me that what we did is a far cry from the impressive efforts undertaken by qualified scientists. But we did what we could, just to make sure we weren't imagining the rug's travels.

We dragged the rug back to the far left of the kitchen and did a second test over a longer time. This time, the kitchen rug moved ten and a half inches in four days. I kept track of the movement throughout.

Saturday, Nov. 8:

Morning [I didn't record the precise time initially, but we placed it after breakfast around seven thirty a.m.]. Rug is flush against wall.

Sunday, Nov. 9:

11 a.m. Rug is 2⅜ inches from wall.

Monday, Nov. 10:

10:30 a.m. Rug is 2⅞ inches from wall.
1:36 p.m. Rug is 3¼ inches from wall.

7:12 p.m. Rug is 4¼ inches from wall.

8:15 p.m. Rug is 4½ inches from wall.

Tuesday, Nov. 11:

8:27 a.m. Rug is 5 inches from wall.

9:30 p.m. Rug is 7⅝ inches from wall.

Wednesday, Nov. 12:

7:30 a.m. Rug is 10½ inches from wall.

The rug ultimately bumped into the corner molding on the right side of the kitchen cabinets and began to curl up the side of the molding, just as the rug in Sun Valley had done when it wandered up the side of the hearth. Only this rug in Napa was moving from left to right, in the direction of the library. It was headed for Max's books.

A week later we had the exact same experience with the rug in our Napa master bedroom. This was also a heavy rug that measured six by eight feet and sat on a thick pad. It conducted its little excursion toward a chest of drawers, eventually crossing seven to eight inches of floor space over two days, until it hit the chest. It, too, was moving in the direction of the library.

I called Robin to tell her what had happened. She said she believes all mass has energy, and the hundreds of Max's books that were still in the library had considerable mass. She suggested it might be time to part with Max's books. Not only would this help Max to move on if he was stuck, but she thought it might also stop the strange movement of the rugs.

I wanted to do anything I could to be helpful to Max. If he was caught, I wanted to help him move on. So Jim and I packed up all of Max's books, filling some twenty boxes, and donated them all to the Napa library.

Just like the powdery prints becoming a pattern that repeated itself over three consecutive years, so, too, a pattern was forming with these moving rugs—one in Sun Valley in the summer, two more in Napa three months later. I could not help but feel that Max was working hard to get my attention. It seemed that he wanted me to know that he was still around, still active, although in another form. He was persistent and creative. Each time something new occurred, I thought the same thing: *This is not possible.* But when it repeated I found myself coming to a different conclusion. Maybe Max was stuck. But I think more likely, if it was Max reaching through the veil and prompting these events, he was doing it because he'd promised that he would. I was becoming more and more certain: there's no way our lives end when we die.

I am certain of two other things pertaining to the moving rugs. The first is that I will not be contacted by a prestigious scientific journal wanting to publish the results of our findings. And the second is that some readers will think that Jim and I were imagining the rugs moving or that they were just slipping under our feet somehow. Not so. But I am fully aware of how ridiculous this sounds.

I had an early glimpse of the possible reaction to this story of moving rugs. Our very dear friends Laura Anderson and Van Lemons, both neurosurgeons, had vacation homes a block away from ours in Yountville and a block away from our home in Sacramento. I called to tell them the story about the rugs and to ask if they would like to have the rug from the kitchen. I thought it would behave more like a normal rug if it weren't with me. I felt safe telling them my story because I trusted them and they knew and loved Max. They weren't the kind of people who jump to judge, and they had been through a lot with Tanner and me after Max died. Their son Robbie was a friend of Tanner's, too.

"Maybe the rug would be unaffected if it weren't around me," I earnestly explained.

"Sure, we would love to have it," Laura said.

So I said, "When can Jim and I drop it off?"

Then Van, who has a wicked sense of humor, said, "Don't bother. Just give the rug our address, and I'll leave the door open."

Very funny, I thought. *Ha-ha.*

Happily, with one rug banned for not staying put and with Max's books removed from the house, the other rug apparently decided to go straight. All of Max's things that I just couldn't part with were packed and sent to Sun Valley. We never had any strange occurrences in Napa again.

CHAPTER 14

Am I Going Nuts?

Jim and I had lived in our new home in Sun Valley for only four months of 2008, and as we kicked off the New Year in 2009, we were still coping with what seemed to be an ongoing issue with our lighting system. The lights in the master bathroom would come on in the middle of the night. I would get up and turn them off, and the next morning, they were on again. We assumed it was because they were new, and we asked the electrician who installed them to come over and investigate. He found nothing amiss and looked at us like we were a little nutty. Then one day the lights in the guest bedroom flickered ever so slightly, prompted by nothing. Despite everything that had gone on with lights flickering in Sacramento, I didn't automatically assume this to be a similar mysterious event. Instead, I chose to think it was an electrical malfunction of some sort. Nothing more.

Then one day our construction foreman stopped by to check on us and relayed a story out of the blue that got our attention. He said that when he and his two carpenters were working in the house one day over the previous summer, all the lights flickered throughout. After the flickering, the three of them noticed a dimming of the lights, followed by a very bright level of lighting. He said this was occurring throughout the house, as far as they could tell. Then the lights all went completely out. Just like that, the show was over. What was really odd, he said, was that no one had touched any of the keypads. And as on most days during the summer, he and his carpenters weren't in the habit of using the lights anyway because the sun was brilliant and our home faces directly to the west, with a wall of floor-to-ceiling windows. He also noted that it had happened only that one time. Every other day throughout the construction, the lights behaved normally, meaning they stayed off.

As I was listening to him, I couldn't help noticing how what he was saying and who he was were at opposite poles. If you looked up "construction foreman" in the dictionary, his photo would pop up. Deep voice, tall, broad shoulders, strong arms and legs, masculine...all male. I think he was mystified by what he'd experienced, yet he couldn't discount it, either. He knew it happened. He just couldn't explain it.

A few weeks later, as a part of the moving-in process that wouldn't end, Jim noticed something. The one box of Max's intimate possessions that I kept after he died lay on the floor of the hall coat closet, directly under the master control panel for the house lighting system. We immediately moved the box to our offsite storage unit, and the problems with the lights went away. Was the energy of his belongings here in Sun Valley like the energy of his books in Napa? Were they capable of initiating activity?

I was curious whether the phenomena that had begun in 2004 in Sacramento and had followed me to Napa and the rental in Sun Valley would now materialize here in our new Sun Valley home. The threads had appeared in the living room in September 2008, and the lights had flickered around that same time. Now in March 2009, I had another encounter with Indra's Net. I was taking a bath when I suddenly saw beautiful bright round circles of translucent light filling the entire ceiling above the tub. They were about four inches in diameter and packed together in such a way that each circle was in contact with other circles. They were sparkling and glittery. I moved the water in the tub with my hand to make sure something wasn't reflecting off the water. It wasn't.

These experiences were not intimidating at all. On the contrary, the circles seemed to transmit the same elegance that the golden threads had. The circles lasted about forty-five minutes and then disappeared. Over the next four months, they appeared three more times, but on the walls and ceiling of our master bedroom instead of the bathroom ceiling. I would wake up in the middle of the night, see them, and feel mesmerized by their beauty. I'd awaken Jim, who would grumble slightly, then stop in midsentence to join me in staring at the delicate and exquisite pageantry. We had absolutely no idea what it meant. But we knew how we felt when we saw it. We were enchanted.

In the first week of June 2010, Jim and I were excited to welcome a new puppy into our lives. Blue was an eight-week-old yellow Lab we acquired from a breeder in Florida through one of Jim's good friends who is a veterinarian. Jim flew Blue home in a small kennel stored under the airline seat in front of him. Their flight made three stops, and Jim looked exhausted by the time he got back to Sun Valley.

We called him Blue the Wonder Dog, because he would

proudly leap from the third step of our staircase down to the landing as if he were flying. He seemed pleased with his new home. On his first night he slept on my stomach in an inflatable bed because I wanted to bond with him. He didn't cry, and we snuggled all night long.

These were some of the finest days of my life. I was contentedly married to Jim and very grateful for our loving relationship. Tanner was thriving at UCLA with his academics, rugby, and fraternity, and I was taking pleasure in all that Sun Valley had to offer.

The Wood River Valley, where Sun Valley is located, is one of the most beautiful places in the country. An hour away by small plane is the Frank Church–River of No Return Wilderness Area, the largest wilderness area in the lower forty-eight states. In Sacramento I had been a walker. Now I was a hiker. Starting at five thousand feet and hiking to seventy-five hundred feet is a considerably different experience from walking. I was hiking with Jim and Blue the Wonder Dog in five mountain ranges within minutes from our home. Mountain lakes are everywhere. A trailhead fifteen minutes from our home could take a hiker all the way to Canada without seeing civilization.

Simply put, I loved the freedom from the relentless responsibility of running a newspaper. And not just because of the outdoors. Sun Valley is home to both a superb symphony and a nationally recognized writers' conference. I was as happy as or happier than I'd ever been in my life.

But exploring the realm of spirituality remained a priority. So when I ran into Traci Ireland in town, I scheduled an appointment with her to discover what she practices and believes. I had previously met Traci at the Sun Valley Wellness Festival, an annual event sponsored by the Sun Valley Wellness

Institute. Traci opened the festival with an outdoor fire cere-mony dedicated to bringing the community together. According to their website, the institute is "an Idaho nonprofit corporation founded in 2005 to provide education on health and wellness through programs and events, including the Sun Valley Well-ness Festival." The festival bills itself as "an annual gathering of the top speakers and practitioners of mind-body-spirit and environmental wellness." Past speakers include Deepak Chopra, Ram Dass, Dr. Jill Bolte Taylor, Marianne Williamson, Byron Katie, Robert F. Kennedy Jr., and, more recently, Dr. Eben Alex-ander. The mission is to "inspire positive change."

Traci is a youthful, athletic woman in her early forties with an immaculate complexion, straight white teeth, and bright brown eyes. What I felt immediately when I met her was how at peace she seemed. Traci was raised on a farm/ranch in south-western South Dakota between the Pine Ridge and Rosebud Indian Reservations in a very loving and supportive Christian family. She earned a bachelor's degree in chemical engineering at the South Dakota School of Mines and Technology and worked as an engineer for eight years but became increasingly disenchanted.

So she moved to Ketchum, Idaho, and became part owner in Chapter One Bookstore. Eventually, her growing spiritual awareness and desire to be of service led her to Alberto Villoldo, Ph.D., a medical anthropologist and psychologist who had founded the Four Winds Society. Dr. Villoldo studied with shamans in Peru for more than thirty years and has written several bestselling books, including *Shaman, Healer, Sage, The Four Insights, Courageous Dreaming,* and *Power Up Your Brain.*

Traci completed the core Light Body School offered through the Four Winds Society in 2006, mainly in Park City, Utah, with additional master's classes through 2008. "The Peruvian shamanic healing practices are thousands of years old," Traci said. "What Alberto teaches is 'pure' in the sense that when the conquistadors arrived in Peru, the shamans retreated to the mountains, where they were able to maintain their traditions uncompromised."

When I asked Traci what had attracted her to Dr. Villoldo's teachings, she replied, "I have a scientific background and was feeling that the earth is shifting. Growing up near Indian reservations, I knew that native people have much to teach us about living in balance within and without. Alberto weaves the spiritual and the scientific by acknowledging the physics behind how we create our own reality, while, at the same time, returning to ancient methods of healing and honoring of our Mother Earth." Traci has traveled to Peru three times, where she worked with the native shamans and visited sacred sites for ceremonies and meditation. She describes her experiences in Peru as "priceless."

The practice taught by Dr. Villoldo incorporates the healing techniques of Peruvian shamans in the form of a medicine wheel. The goal is to heal people and bring about a "clear, luminous" field of energy to surround them for the purpose of addressing any issue a person might be facing, such as grief, guilt, or sadness. I was mainly curious whether her teachings would shed light on the powdery handprints, the moving rugs, the luminous threads, the flickering lights, and, most recently, the translucent balls of light.

I had several sessions with Traci. In the initial one, I visited Traci at a home not far from ours where she was staying. Entering the sun-filled living room, for some reason I found myself focusing on the bookshelves near the sofa instead of the spectacular views of the mountains seen through the large bay window. There on crowded shelves I saw two items that stood out from all the others. One was the book *Meditations* by the Roman emperor Marcus Aurelius. This is the same book I had arbitrarily pulled off the shelves in our Napa library and in doing so had discovered Max's dog-eared page with the quote "Despise not death, but welcome it, for nature wills it like all else." How many people keep a copy of this book? Why, out of all the books on the shelves during this session with Traci, did this single volume catch my eye? Was Max letting me know he was there with me?

The second item nestled among the books was a Native American doll. With her dark black hair, hard plastic face, and yellow suede outfit, she was identical in size and features to one my dad gave me when I was about five or six years old. We had been on a camping trip out west, and he bought it for me at a tourist shop near Yellowstone Park. I had not seen another one in all these years. And now here she was. For whatever reason, seeing her instantly made me think of Dad. Was he, like Max, making his presence known?

Traci began her work with me by calling in several archetypes from the animal kingdom. She told me that the jaguar "showed up" during our session and that the jaguar is a protector that allows us to walk in peace. The jaguar teaches us how to walk across the bridge between this world and the world of spirit. It guides us along the way beyond fear and death. I found that to be quite relevant, as it fit with the spiritual journey I felt I was on. She indicated that this jaguar would remain with me, watching over me and serving as an ally on my path.

At another session, Traci told me she had a visceral feeling that Max's spirit had, indeed, remained over the years, but she felt he was preparing to move "home." She said it was healing for both Max and me to know he could "cross the bridge" to the other side and meet his greeters. She indicated that it didn't mean he would stay put, but he would find his home. And she said together she and I would concentrate on "passing his spirit forward with good and loving attention," which is what we did in our session and what I practiced on my own at home as well with prayer and meditation.

These experiences with Traci were a part of the due diligence I was conducting by exposing myself to philosophies that could challenge my thinking. I'll never know whether Max's spirit moved across "the bridge," but it was an enlightening experience to learn from Traci about ancient Peruvian healing practices.

In July, Jim and I flew to a ranch in northern Idaho that he and some other partners share. We were going to celebrate our second wedding anniversary. I love it there, and we've made it an annual event each July. The Flying B Ranch on the Middle Fork of the Salmon River can be accessed only by backpacking, horseback riding, floating the river, or flying in a small airplane. It's thirty-eight miles southwest of Salmon, Idaho, in the heart of the Frank Church–River of No Return Wilderness. Our entertainment is hiking and horseback riding, horseshoes and checkers. Meals are served family style and announced with the clanging of an iron rod against a triangle, just like in the old Westerns. At night we can hear the sounds of the river rushing by the back of our cabin.

After a restful few days, we returned to our home in Sun Valley. Soon after we arrived, Jim walked into our den. I was right around the corner in the kitchen (not cooking, never cooking) when I heard him say aloud to himself, "What's this?"

I circled back around the hallway to the den and peered in so I could see for myself what he was looking at. There, on the arm of one of our three gold suede club chairs, was a very large footprint. That's right. A very large footprint.

I thought I'd seen it all. Apparently not. Slightly unnerved, my lips involuntarily squeezing into a rather tight slit, I found myself doing an impersonation of a composed person.

With a resolute, flat voice I said, "What? You mean the footprint on the chair?"

It was almost comical. Only it really wasn't. Was I going nuts? Were we both going nuts? Whatever this was, it seemed to be following me. Our Sun Valley home was the fourth house (including the rental we lived in while we were building this home) where we witnessed remarkable events. More than just a pattern, this was a very persistent pattern extending over six years. And it wasn't as if these were the ordinary kinds of events you often read about in literature on the mystical realm. I could understand lights flickering, doors closing, clocks stopping. These are well documented. But powdery handprints appearing from nowhere on mirrors, rugs moving of their own volition, and a large footprint on the arm of our chair? Hardly normal.

I looked back down at the footprint and back up at Jim, who was standing just in front of the chair, transfixed. "What do you think it is?" I asked.

"I have no idea," he responded.

The image was significantly oversize, similar to the bigger-than-life handprint on the bathroom mirror in Sacramento. From the view of someone sitting in the chair, the print was on the left arm. Someone facing the chair, like we were, saw it on the right side. There was nothing on either side of the chair—it was situated in the middle of the room, facing the other two chairs directly opposite. The ceiling is about fifteen feet above, with no light fixture other than recessed lighting over the chair. In other words, there is no reason anyone would need or want to stand on the chair.

Then we noticed something even more peculiar. The print of the bare foot was a left footprint, with the heel at the front end of the arm and the toes pointing to the back of the chair. This means that the corresponding right foot would be dangling in midair. I couldn't help thinking this was an impossible feat—or is that feet? But I digress.

"Are you sure Veronica [our housekeeper] wasn't here?" I asked.

"She comes on Wednesday, never on a weekend, and her foot is about half the size of this one," Jim reminded me.

I knew I was just looking for easy answers, rational explanations.

We took photos and decided that we would observe this footprint carefully over the next forty-eight hours. What was so striking was that, unlike the handprints, the footprint changed in placement and composition over the two days we watched it. The footprint shifted slightly from left to right, ending up looking as if it was going to slip off the chair. It also developed a thin line down the middle of the foot that was not there the first day. And a slight extension began to form off the big toe.

The only way I can describe my feelings at the time is by way of analogy. The combined effect of all the phenomena over the past six years made me feel as if someone were speaking to me, but in a foreign language. And the message seemed to be consequential. But since I knew only a few of the words, I was struggling to translate and understand the message. The language and communications were animated and incredibly creative. Why were they so hard to interpret? I had never been more curious, more puzzled, more provoked than I was then.

This was a turning point. Jim and I agreed that we needed to stop being reactive and start being more proactive. We wanted to focus our efforts and take the initiative to investigate more seriously what was occurring.

"Some people can just accept things and move through their lives," he said. "I'm not one of those. I have to understand and I want you to understand what this means."

This was the moment I decided that I had to take these extraordinary events to someone who could really help me understand them and put them in perspective. I had to know what I didn't know. I had to break the language barrier.

CHAPTER 15

I'm Not Nuts

The footprint was an evocative testament to the fact that the otherworldly events were not subsiding. After wrestling with the accumulation of phenomena over multiple years, I was now dealing with a spontaneously appearing footprint that altered itself over the course of two days.

This ultimately led to the decision to meet face-to-face with an authority in the field of parapsychology to gain some insight. I wanted perspective and needed to fill the gap in my knowledge. I was determined to get serious about understanding the science behind this phenomenon, including continuing to learn about the study of consciousness. I called Dr. Wendland to ask whom he might recommend I meet with to pursue my questions. He offered to introduce me to Dr. Dean Radin, his coauthor in the experiment on conscious intention affecting the pattern of light. Jim agreed to come with me, and together we planned our trip to interview Dr. Radin in Northern California.

My mind was racing as we traveled from Sun Valley to Petaluma, California, to meet with Dr. Radin, who is chief scientist
at the Institute of Noetic Sciences (IONS). The institute's
name is taken from the Greek word *nous*, which means "intuitive mind" or "inner knowing." IONS is dedicated to exploring
the potential and the power of consciousness. The scientists
there also conduct research in phenomena that do not yet fit
prevailing scientific models. This seemed to be a near perfect
match for what I was seeking.

Apollo 14 astronaut Edgar Mitchell, who holds a Ph.D. in
aeronautics and astronautics from MIT, founded IONS in 1973.
Dr. Mitchell had an overwhelming visceral and majestic experience on his trip back from the moon that ultimately led to a
passion to understand more. As he later put it, "It began with
a breathtaking experience of seeing planet earth floating in
the vastness of space. The presence of divinity became almost
palpable, and I knew that life in the universe was not just an
accident based on random processes. This knowledge came to
me directly—noetically. Clearly, the universe had meaning and
direction."

In advance of my meeting with Dr. Radin at the institute's research offices near downtown Petaluma, he had kindly
arranged for a tour of IONS's experiential retreat center outside
of town. The two hundred acres of beautiful pastoral land seem
far more remote than the mere forty miles from San Francisco
would suggest. And I mean "pastoral" quite literally. Hundreds
of sheep and goats graze on the property, and it's very quiet and
peaceful.

Our tour was conducted by Lisa VanderBoom, an attrac-
tive, energetic, smart young woman clearly dedicated to the
organization's mission. It didn't take long for us to begin sharing

personal spiritual experiences. As she explained, the facility is used primarily for training and workshops and can house up to one hundred overnight guests. Classes are available from the institute or other similar organizations.

After the tour, Jim and I drove to the research offices to meet with Dr. Radin. He is an intense but quiet man with an obviously great intellect and sharp wit. He reminds me of the quintessential professor. It's also not too hard to imagine him as a concertmaster, since he was a professional concert violinist for five years. He is a careful listener and generous with his insights and his time.

It was clear from his amiable interaction with the staff that he is highly regarded. As we were starting our meeting at his conference table, an associate stuck his head in the door and asked if we would like some lights on for our meeting. "Oh, sure, good idea," Dr. Radin said. Maybe that's the classic absentminded professor in him. Whatever it was, I liked him right away because he was unassuming, casual, and confident, not easily impressed and not needing to impress.

Dr. Radin has an undergraduate degree in electrical engineering from the University of Massachusetts Amherst and a master's degree in electrical engineering and a Ph.D. in educational psychology from the University of Illinois. He began his career doing industrial research with AT&T Bell Labs, but he knew early on that he wanted to focus on consciousness.

He came to national prominence in 1996 when *The New York Times Magazine* published an article about him. In 1997 he published his first book, *The Conscious Universe*. In 2006 he followed with a second book, *Entangled Minds*. His latest book, published in 2013, is *Supernormal: Science, Yoga, and the Evidence for Extraordinary Psychic Abilities*. He also cofounded a Silicon Valley think tank with computer scientist Richard Shoup called Boundary Institute. Dr. Radin was elected president of the Parapsychological Association in 1988, 1993, 1998, and 2005.

Dr. Radin is so highly respected by his peers that some might argue he is the dean of parapsychology (pun intended; sorry, I couldn't help myself). I had arranged for this meeting in great part to help get at specific questions that were gnawing at me: Are my experiences highly unusual relative to others'? How do I make sense of them scientifically, if at all? What does the field of parapsychology cover? What kind of research and analysis is being conducted by Dr. Radin? What about his take on consciousness? And secretly, deep down, I have to admit, I was hoping to find out whether or not I was going nuts!

We started our session with a conversation about his pioneering work in meta-analysis. With his permission I recorded our conversation and kept notes throughout. I had learned from my previous sessions with Dr. Wendland, Dr. de la Herran, and Loyd Auerbach that the information I was gathering was not only unfamiliar, it was sometimes intimidating. Listening carefully was imperative.

I learned that meta-analysis is a process that combines the results of experiments of similar kinds and analyzes them statistically for patterns. Dr. Radin did this work at Princeton Engineering Anomalies Research (PEAR), which was founded in 1979 (and given its innocuous-sounding name to avoid the stigma of parapsychology) by Robert Jahn, a Ph.D. in physics from Princeton University, and his associate Dr. Brenda Dunne. PEAR operated until 2007.

Dr. Jahn wanted to study the quantum physics hypothesis advanced by Niels Bohr, who had proposed that no one could ever know the precise location of an electron until it was measured. (This was the same theory that Dr. Wendland had explained to me as the Copenhagen interpretation.) The basic premise is that what actually determines location is the observer. After years of investigations, the PEAR team discovered that humans could, indeed, affect what would ordinarily be a random outcome by concentrating on a preferred outcome.

Because Dr. Radin's research spanned a number of disciplines and he was interested in parapsychology, in 1987 Dr. Jahn invited him to coordinate a program that included the PEAR lab. Among Dr. Radin's responsibilities was to analyze the results of more than eight hundred experiments.

Using meta-analysis, Dr. Radin came up with a startling finding: the odds that the human mind was affecting outcome were better than a trillion to one.

He is not the only one who has done meta-analysis of these kinds of experiments. "Many such meta-analyses have been published since the 1980s, as I describe in my books," Dr. Radin said. "These have significantly advanced the evidential support for psi."

I learned from Dr. Radin that the term "psi" (pronounced *sigh*; also, the twenty-third letter of the Greek alphabet) was coined in 1942 by a British psychologist named Robert Thouless to refer to all psychic phenomena. Telepathy, or mind-to-mind connection, is one of the common psi occurrences. Others are clairvoyance, or perceiving distant objects or events; precognition, or perceiving future events; and psychokinesis, when the mind affects matter. Psi also includes near-death experiences, out-of-body experiences, psychic healing, after-death communications, apparitions, and other paranormal activities.

Another famous meta-analysis of a type of telepathy test

known as a ganzfeld experiment found that controlled laboratory evidence of telepathy was at least ten times more likely to be valid than the results of multiple studies indicating that aspirin is useful in avoiding a heart attack. "Curiously," Dr. Radin pointed out to me, "millions of Americans dutifully take their aspirin each day, while skeptics continue to doubt the effects of consciousness."

In his own studies of psi phenomena, Dr. Radin developed a unique way to measure premonition by connecting research volunteers to devices that measure heart rate and blood pressure and the degree to which skin conducts electricity. Using photographs in a sequence designed to emotionally stimulate the volunteers, the study demonstrated that the volunteers were able to anticipate what they were about to see.

I asked Dr. Radin to define the nature of consciousness according to his research. Based on numerous experiments, Dr. Radin speculates that consciousness has at least five general characteristics.

First, consciousness not only exists; it extends beyond individuals and has quantum properties that affect the likelihood of events occurring.

Second, consciousness injects order into systems in proportion to its strength.

Third, the strength of consciousness fluctuates according to the level of focus.

As Dr. Radin touches on this third point, I think about focus in everyday life and how that focus translates into results, whether it's a disciplined and practiced star athlete, musician, doctor, artist, or business executive. When we as humans focus on what we want and work to achieve it, we can and often do produce results that go beyond the norm. Does it work the same after we die? Does extreme focus create exceptional results? Is this persistent activity due to a dedicated focus in another realm from Max?

Fourth, groups have a kind of shared consciousness when all members are focused on an event or object. Dr. Radin was among the first to demonstrate this collective consciousness. Using the O. J. Simpson murder trial, in which half a billion viewers worldwide tuned in to see the acquittal in 1995, he was able to show a subtle but significant change in the randomness of random-number generators that had been placed in a variety of locations. The conclusion was that the effects of combined consciousness can be measured and that distance is irrelevant. Similar changes have since been recorded with other major world events: the tragic attacks of September 11, 2001, and the election of Barack Obama as president in 2008, among them.

If this is evidence of collective consciousness and consciousness unaffected by distance, then why would it be limited to human beings and to the physical geography of the earth? Isn't it possible that the same collective consciousness could be spirit bound as well as earthbound? Simply put, is consciousness unencumbered from all physical boundaries? Taking it one step further, when we die, do we join a collective consciousness? Can we band together and by setting intention form the "likelihood of events occurring," as Dr. Radin puts it, across the boundaries of life and death?

The fifth characteristic of consciousness identified by Dr. Radin is that physical systems respond to focused consciousness by becoming more ordered. Dr. Radin says the evidence indicates that intention and attention somehow shape reality. "Strong intention works space-time in such a way as to bring you and things out there into the same orbit," he said.

I found myself pausing to take a deep breath. I've wondered all along if the strong intention that Max might be extending from the spirit side to this side would have persisted had it not been for the attention I gave it. Over the course of my journey, I had developed the intention to pay attention to the extraordinary events I was experiencing because I was deeply curious and committed to trying to make sense of what they meant. Said another way, had I been a partner to Max in keeping these occurrences alive? Between the two of us, had we worked space-time in such a way as to bring ourselves into the same orbit across the boundaries of life and death? Is that even possible?

I was curious about synchronicity since I had read about C. G. Jung's theory of synchronicity in Dr. Radin's *The Conscious Universe* and felt that I might have experienced some synchronicities myself. According to *Merriam-Webster's*, synchronicity is "the coincidental occurrence of events and especially psychic events (as similar thoughts in widely separated persons or a mental image of an unexpected event before it happens) that seem related but are not explained by conventional mechanisms of causality—used especially in the psychology of C. G. Jung." I asked Dr. Radin to elaborate on the concept.

In response to my question, Dr. Radin told me an amazing personal story about what appears to be either an incredible case of coincidence or a strong case of synchronicity. In early 2000, when he and Richard Shoup created the Boundary Institute in Palo Alto, rents were so expensive that they ended up in an office park in Los Altos in a small place among many other small professional companies. "We didn't even have a name on our door yet, but I was already dreaming about how to equip and furnish our office and lab," Dr. Radin said. "I was imagining all the things that we would need and how I would lay it out."

After commuting to the new office for several weeks, he decided to take a different route, which led him to notice a company called PSI Quest Lab right next door. "I just assumed it was Personnel Services Incorporated, but I couldn't understand why they would need a lab. My curiosity got the better of me, so one day I walked by and looked through the windows. I didn't see anyone at all," he said.

He passed by a number of times but never saw anyone in that office. He continued busily selecting equipment and designing a layout for his lab.

"Another week went by, and as I was leaving, I looked again through the window of PSI Quest Lab. This time there was someone inside. So I knocked on the door with the intention of introducing myself, and a gentleman came to the door. As he opened the door he got a look of shock on his face. I thought he might be having a heart attack, but he didn't say anything. I didn't know what to do because normally when someone opens a door, he or she says something. So to fill the silence I said, 'Hi, I am at the office next door.' But he interrupted me and said, 'You're Dean Radin.'"

Dr. Radin had no idea who the man was.

"Well, it turned out that this was a private company started by an ex-Apple employee who was one of the original Power-Book developers. He had cashed out and was doing the same kind of research we were doing. He said he had always wanted to do psi research.

"He told me he had been in his lab every day using Tibetan dream yoga trying to bring me into existence. In Tibetan dream yoga you put yourself into a kind of trance. He said he was trying to will me to show up and join his board of directors to help with fund-raising. You can imagine the astonishment. I actually showed up. There are very few psi laboratories in the world, and here we were right next door to each other. Then it was my turn to be shocked. He invited me in, and I saw that his laboratory was exactly the same laboratory I had been dreaming about in the space next door."

This kind of synchronicity, when things occur coincidentally, has real meaning, Dr. Radin said.

"It works if one or more persons have desire at some level," he said. "He had manifested something on his side of the synchronicity because he was imagining that he needed me, just as I was imagining that I needed a certain kind of laboratory. Our orbits arranged themselves so our free-will decision led to me opening the door and our meeting."

With the prevalence of stories such as his, mine, and others he has heard, Dr. Radin has a hard time understanding the lack of commitment to the study of psi phenomena.

He explained that virtually all the founders of modern physics have questioned the role of consciousness in a physical universe. I learned that chief among them was Werner Heisenberg, whom Dr. Wendland had mentioned in our sessions. Along with Werner Heisenberg, Dr. Radin cited Erwin Schrödinger and Albert Einstein as questioning the role of consciousness. And there are numerous contemporary scientists who have questioned the role of consciousness in a physical universe. Yet Dr. Radin has found only a handful of studies on consciousness that have been published in current mainstream physics journals. In fact, at any given time there are fewer than fifty conventionally trained doctoral-level scientists in the world engaged in full-time psi research.

"If all the funds for cancer research spent in a single year were instead spent in one day, then the comparative funding for psi research, worldwide and throughout history, would consume a mere forty-three seconds of that day," he said. He told me that it was proposed some years ago that if just 1 percent of national research funds were devoted to psi phenomena, that would be several hundred million times more than what was currently being allotted.

I asked him what he would do if he had more funding.

"I would create advanced education programs to get students and scientists up to speed on the available evidence, and I would continue studying the nature of mind-matter interaction, as I've been doing for some years now."

Dr. Radin thinks future work in this field depends largely on public demand. If interest is high, funds will flow into research. "If people are ambivalent about psi research, then it will continue to lie on the fringe, and we will not advance to the next stage. It's that simple," he said.

As frustrating as this is, Dr. Radin maintains a healthy and humorous attitude. In this vein, he described how mainstream science accepts new ideas in five stages.

"In stage one, skeptics proclaim a new idea is impossible and violates the laws of science," he said. "In stage two, skeptics proclaim the idea is possible but uninteresting, and the effects are so weak that no one would care. In stage three, mainstream scientists begin to realize the idea is important and the effects are stronger than previously thought. By stage four, the same skeptics announce they thought of the idea first. And finally in stage five, hardly anyone remembers that the idea was once considered to be controversial, and those few who do remember have forgotten why."

He sees us in the transition from stage one to stage two. We clearly have a long way to go, but it will take more research and, equally important, a more open attitude on the part of the general public.

As Dr. Radin said, "Most people say, 'I'll believe it when I see it.' Actually, you'll see it when you believe it."

As I sat in Dr. Radin's office and showed him my photographs, turning them over one by one on the table, I was reminded again of how these events had affected me. First shock, then a kind of denial mixed with some intrigue, followed by immense curiosity and a drive to learn—for years.

He seemed intrigued by my story and, being the scientist he is, immediately identified some things I should have done: tested the hand images for fingerprints, performed a chemical analysis, conducted a vibration measurement on the floor for the rugs. Of course, he is right. But I didn't spend my life in science; I spent it in newspapers. Luckily that experience kicked in, and I had the foresight to photograph and document what I saw.

"Skeptics will say somebody made those prints, and the rugs and other events were imagined, or you were hallucinating or suffering from grief," Dr. Radin warned. He's probably right. But that's where finding the courage to do the right thing comes in, despite the skeptics and critics. Dr. Radin is a great role model. He has had the courage to advance his research and views in the face of pushback and skepticism from the majority of the scientific community.

Now it was time to ask the question I had come for. Had he seen anything like these handprints before? I assumed that what I had shown him was far outside the norm and would astound him. I could not have been more wrong.

He told me he couldn't think of anything exactly like my experiences, but that he and his colleagues regularly see similar things in the research they conduct—thousands of similar things, in fact. And the clock stopping at 12:44? He said you could write an entire book about clocks stopping for inexplicable reasons associated with emotional events. So after all this time and all the anguish I had been living with, including feeling that I might be, yes, going nuts, I learned that my experiences are not that unusual.

What I thought was extraordinary was, in fact, ordinary. Apparently, paranormal is normal. I just didn't know it. And there's a reason. People are afraid to admit what they have experienced. They're reluctant to speak publicly about what they've experienced for fear of being judged.

I didn't know whether to laugh or cry. Instead of feeling relief that I was not alone in my experiences and therefore not a fruitcake, I was caught totally off guard by a different emotion. I felt ignorant and wondered why I hadn't known about parapsychology and the study of consciousness. Why didn't I know that many people had similar experiences? I was learning a very valuable lesson. It had to do with perspective. Just because people don't talk about something openly doesn't mean it doesn't exist. This is why research and education are imperative. If we persist in being comfortable with our own thoughts and ideas and don't challenge ourselves to stretch, learning new ways of thinking and viewing the world, we can end up both naïve and ignorant.

Jim and I didn't talk as we drove back to our hotel, quietly processing what we had heard. He had the perfect medicine for us: a stroll on the Bodega Bay beach with Blue. Jim threw a ball in the surf for Blue as I sat on a chair and reflected on what I had learned. This meeting had proven to be groundbreaking for me. I had thought my experiences would shock Dr. Radin. But it was the reverse. Instead he blew me away by telling me that my experiences are not uncommon. I sat on the beach wondering what all this meant and how it would affect my perspective going forward.

And then it hit me, as epiphanies often do.

I had lived these past years with a subtle but nagging fear that my exposure to these stunning occurrences meant that somehow I wasn't "normal." Because the events were so strange, I initially stayed quiet. Eventually I shared my experiences, but I was selective in whom I chose to speak with. Bottom line, I didn't want people to think I was nuts. If they did, it might mean that, yes—I was nuts. But now, for the first time, I had confirmation that I wasn't that unusual. In fact, I was normal.

Why didn't I know that such experiences are not rare? I consider myself to be relatively well informed. Why doesn't the general public know this? The fact that many people experience the supernatural world, yet few of us speak up about it, is a cultural and societal issue that deserves consideration. How much better it would be if we all understood that there is nothing wrong with feeling, hearing, or seeing a communication from a loved one who has died.

It was then that I remembered something else that Dr. Radin had written about in his book *The Conscious Universe*. He cites Andrew Greeley, a Catholic priest and a sociologist at the University of Arizona, who in a 1987 survey found that 67 percent of American adults reported having psychic experiences. Greeley also found that many widows who reported contact by their dead husbands had not previously believed in life after death.

According to Greeley, "People who've tasted the paranormal, whether they accept it intellectually or not, are anything but religious nuts or psychiatric cases. They are, for the most part, ordinary Americans, somewhat above the norm in education and intelligence and somewhat less than average in religious involvement."

This was a pivotal moment in my journey, a true turning point with momentous importance. I went from believing my story was extraordinary to realizing that these types of events are happening to many people. In other words, what is in fact extraordinary is the very ordinariness of it.

I realized, sitting in my folding canvas chair on the Bodega Bay beach, watching Jim and Blue play ball, that it was time for me to start talking openly, without shame or embarrassment. From this point forward, I vowed to myself, I would open up not only to those I was interviewing for my research, but to my family and friends as well. And if I could comfort anyone, what a privilege that would be.

It was a breakthrough. I felt free. Liberated. Unshackled.

CHAPTER 16

A Spiritual Awakening

In June 2011, Jim, being the planner that he is, asked me what I wanted for my sixtieth birthday, which was coming up in October. It was a nice gesture on his part, but I wasn't interested in discussing it. It would mean acknowledging I was, in fact, turning sixty years old. Not possible.

I'd spent most of the last eighteen months throwing out every single AARP mailing I received without opening one. Truth is, I found them more than a little annoying. I was in complete denial. But Jim was persistent, so finally one day I said, "Okay, you decide because I can't." It didn't take him long to declare that we were going to Canyon Ranch. He told me that the Ranch (as they call it) was "made" for me, given my interest in nutrition and fitness. And he knew I would like the spiritual aspects of the curriculum.

We had sold our Yountville home and purchased a home in Florida to be near Jim's family, and since we planned on being there in October, we thought we would go to Canyon

Ranch in Lenox, Massachusetts, instead of the original flagship ranch in Tucson. Jim had never seen the autumn leaves in the Northeast, so it seemed like a great way to combine a tour of the region with a stay at the ranch. But prior to our trip, Vermont suffered a major flood, and the hotels we had reserved were no longer available. "Let's go to Tucson instead," Jim cheerfully suggested.

I revisited the Canyon Ranch website and quickly found myself envisioning wide-open skies and breathtaking canyons, the allure of the Southwest and the magic of the desert. I began to imagine the culture of the Native Americans. Besides, Tucson represented the soul of the original concept created in 1978, when Enid and Mel Zuckerman cofounded Canyon Ranch. In the thirties and forties it was a working ranch; then in the forties and fifties it became a dude ranch. The Zuckermans purchased it and transformed it by refurbishing the old buildings and enhancing the landscape, capturing the timeless spirit of the land.

I was sold. We changed our reservations.

As October approached, I became more excited. And I was reminded of how lucky I was to have Jim, who has always been so generous and thoughtful. This was his idea, and I was seeing the wisdom of it at last. I started packing my bags, which was easier for a trip to the desert. Workout clothes, T-shirts, and shorts. No makeup. Maybe this sixty-years-old thing was not so bad.

I received the brochure and began planning my options. On the fun side, I would finally have a chance to learn yoga and tai chi. I'd been talking about taking yoga classes since I retired in 2008, but to no avail. Now I had my opportunity! At long last, the dreaded flab on my triceps and tummy would be attacked at the Ranch. And why not take the "Hands on Cooking" classes, since I had never cooked a day in my life? Well, no, wait a minute. That was pushing it. I decided to stick with exercise and the body redo. Classes on healthy eating, better breathing practices, Pilates, core conditioning, stretching, strength training, and skin care to go along with the yoga and tai chi. I was expecting this visit to turn back the clock at least ten years, or at least transform me into a more youthful sixty.

On the more serious side, I checked out the spiritual offerings and was delighted to see numerous choices. Classes for spiritual guidance, meditation, healing, and aligning body, mind, and spirit were listed. The curriculum offered Eastern and Western spiritual traditions and a full staff of practitioners to help with cultivating a "spiritual existence," determining a spiritual path, or giving assistance in "integrating spirituality into your daily life." There were "intuitive tools and guidance" available. The more I read, the more excited I got. This was a unique opportunity, and I couldn't wait!

The Ranch seemed magical from the moment we set foot on the property. I was stirred by the peace and tranquility of the desert. The sky was a deep blue, and the air felt warm and dry. I decided to take another look at the brochure to see what specific classes I might take while we were there.

Sitting down in our suite with the list of offerings for the week, I made my selections. I was especially looking forward to the deep meditation session and the soul coach session. Three classes I made sure to boycott: "Embracing Aging," "Memory Fitness," and "Bingo." Even when I turn ninety, I'm not taking those.

Meanwhile, Jim, who was encouraging my spiritual focus, had scheduled every hour of every day, taking "Golf Full Swing

Tips," followed by "Cardio Golf," followed by "Golf Short Game Tips," followed by "Golf Clinic: Bunkers," followed by "Golf Clinic: Putting." I could go on, but you get the picture.

My first session was entitled "Cultivating Inner Peace." The practitioner talked about the alignment of our outside lives with our souls. She encouraged me to listen to my heart and explore and investigate the spiritual path. "The path chooses you, so listen," she said.

She told me the soul has two purposes: to learn and to teach. Her advice was to listen, be still, and trust. When discussing the "source," she said our wisdom is in our heart. The qualities there are from the divine, and they include wisdom, trust, strength, courage, patience, love, gratitude, protection, peace, and, most of all, forgiveness.

In a later one-on-one session I was led through a deep, concentrated meditation exercise, much like a prayer. I was told to breathe slowly and to quiet my body, focusing heavily on the "universe." The instructor asked me, "What word do you want to use for the source of love? Jesus? God? Buddha? It's up to you."

I have no idea why this popped into my head, but the phrase I chose for the exercise was "The One." We repeated it together. All I could feel was the sound of "The One" as a vibration, an endless tone or capacity. Things began to melt and soften. I was moved by how something so simple and pure could be this rich and rewarding.

After the session, I was walking across the grounds and stopped at a fountain in the center quad. I found myself staring at the fountain. My sense of time evaporated. I felt no separation between the rest of the universe and me. I had a sense of absolute "knowingness" tied to the light from the sun shining through the fountain. I didn't know whether this was a "cosmic consciousness" moment, but what I did know was that the serenity I felt was rare. I had no doubt that there was something sacred about Canyon Ranch.

One evening as we were leaving dinner and walking through the lobby, Jim asked if I had noticed the eight p.m. session with Dr. Gary Schwartz, a professor at the University of Arizona. "He's going to be discussing his latest research on the role of spirit in health and everyday life. You ought to go," Jim said.

I did, and I asked Jim to come with me. Dr. Schwartz also serves as the Canyon Ranch director of development of healing energy services and collaborates on biofield science and energy healing research. He is a very smart, funny man, and he's a whirlwind of energy. His enthusiasm is infectious. He has a wonderful talent for communicating novel ideas in a way that is readily understood. As he paced the room that evening, the dozen or so of us there with him were captivated.

I listened intently as Dr. Schwartz spoke about the divine energy of healing, his experiments with it, and the relationship of science and spirit. He asked, "Is there a greater spiritual reality?" He said he believes that those who have died care as much about us as we do about them. He went on to suggest that his mission in life is to provide scientific evidence of spirit through his work.

What a gift to have the opportunity to hear from a professor and lecturer devoted to the study of the afterlife. As we were leaving the session, Jim suggested that I try to meet with Dr. Schwartz. After the class I introduced myself, and we ended up talking for several hours as I told him about Max and my experiences. He invited me to attend another of his sessions in two days, this one devoted to enhancing personal energy awareness.

After the second class, Dr. Schwartz was kind enough to give me more of his time. I walked with him to his car, and he gave me a copy of his most recent book, *The Sacred Promise*. He asked if I had thought of telling my story about Max more broadly, perhaps by writing about it. He suggested I could give a voice to others to speak up about their experiences. I told him I didn't know. I was still learning, still exploring, still researching, and I wasn't sure where my journey would take me. In other words, what I knew was that I didn't know enough.

Right handprint appears on the bathroom mirror of my home in Sacramento, California, on May 8, 2005.

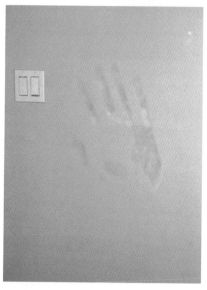

Agnes Olson, my
grandmother, circa 1912.

Axel Olson, my
grandfather, circa 1912.

Margaret and Elvin
Olson, my parents, 1944.

Tanner, Max, and me, Sacramento, 2000.

Tanner and Max, Half Moon Bay, California, 2002.

Max and me, Yosemite, California, 2003.

The full photo was taken in Portofino, Italy, in July 2005.

This highlighted image shows the letters MAX between Tanner and me on a boat in the background.

Angels appear on the bathroom mirror of my home in Sacramento on May 8, 2006, the second anniversary of Max's death.

Tanner and me at a Sacramento Kings game, Sacramento, 2006.

Left handprint appears on the bathroom mirror of my home in Sacramento on May 6, 2007, in the week of the third anniversary of Max's death.

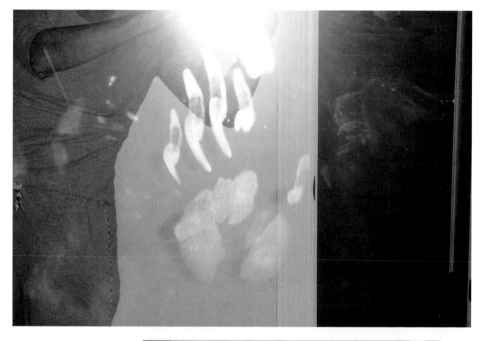

Tom Philp (far left) accepts the Pulitzer Prize for editorial writing for *The Sacramento Bee* in May 2005. Here we are with colleagues at Columbia University in New York.

Renée Byer and me in *The Sacramento Bee* newsroom celebrating the news that Renée had won the Pulitzer Prize for feature photography in April 2007.

Jim and me at our wedding in Sun Valley, Idaho, July 2008.

The initial test of the moving kitchen rug in our Napa home on November 6, 2008.

Follow-up test of the moving kitchen rug in our Napa home on November 8, 2008.

The moving master bedroom rug in our Napa home in mid-November 2008.

A footprint appears on a suede club chair in our Sun Valley, Idaho, home in July 2010.

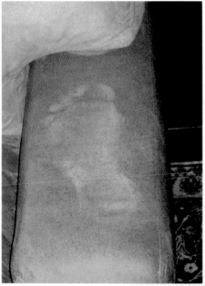

These two photos show the footprint and its shift.

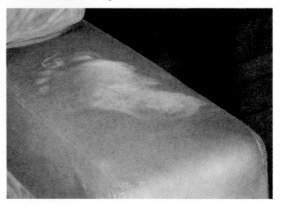

My mother and me on Easter morning in the backyard of our home in Hamilton, Ohio, 1959. The baby in the stroller is my sister, Signe.

"Max" bridge, Cambridge, Nebraska, August 2012.

Besler sign, Cambridge, Nebraska, August 2012.

CHAPTER 17

Near-Death Experiences: Evidence of an Afterlife

What I had understood so far from Dr. Wendland and Dr. Radin was that the nearly universal scientific consensus defined consciousness as the product of brain process. This, of course, made the proposition that the handprints and footprint were initiated by Max null and void. In other words, what had happened was not scientifically possible. But I was not about to give up.

I kept hearing about the neurosurgeon Dr. Eben Alexander and his book, *Proof of Heaven*, so I bought a copy and read it. I learned that he had a near-death experience that led to a change in his traditional view of consciousness. Previously believing, like most members of the scientific community, that consciousness is a product of brain function, he now believed consciousness existed separately. Dr. Alexander was a featured speaker at the Forever Family Foundation meeting I attended, so I not only heard him give his talk, but I spoke with him individually. Mainly I was interested in his view of consciousness as a scientist now that he had abandoned the traditional thinking.

In *Proof of Heaven*, Dr. Alexander recounts in great detail "the strangest, most beautiful world I'd ever seen" while in a coma during a rare illness. During his near-death experience, he maintains that the part of his brain that controls thought and emotion was not functioning. This convinced him that what he experienced in his altered state was heaven. He was in this state for seven days until he recovered.

Following his presentation I spoke with him and explained my situation, that I had embarked on researching the topic of our consciousness surviving death because of what had happened with Max. I asked him, "How do you define consciousness?"

He told me that in his view consciousness exists first and foremost as the "prime thing in our universe." He confirmed what I had read in his book, that he had reversed his previous belief that the brain is the generator of consciousness and believes instead that consciousness is independent of the brain. He believes that near-death reports are often dismissed as evidence because they are personal and anecdotal. But that doesn't make them invalid, he pointed out.

Meeting and speaking with Dr. Alexander prompted me to look further into near-death experiences (commonly called NDEs). I called Dr. Radin and asked him to refer me to the authoritative figure in the field. He introduced me to Dr. Bruce Greyson, who was kind enough to invite me to meet with him at his office in Charlottesville, Virginia. What I would soon discover is that there is an abundance of documented accounts of NDEs, and their remarkable consistency adds up to the strongest evidence we have that consciousness exists outside the brain.

While my experiences weren't NDEs, I was hoping to learn from Dr. Greyson's research whether consciousness survives the body after death. I hoped this might give me insight into whether Max still existed in some form and whether he was trying to communicate with me.

My interview with Dr. Greyson would turn out to be one of the most emotional of my journey. Dr. Greyson is the Carlson Professor Emeritus of Psychiatry and Neurobehavioral Sciences at the University of Virginia in Charlottesville. He is also the former director of the Division of Perceptual Studies in UVA's School of Medicine.

His background is impressive. He received his bachelor's degree in psychology from Cornell University and his M.D. from the State University of New York Upstate College of Medicine. He taught psychiatry at the University of Michigan and the University of Connecticut, where he was clinical chief of psychiatry. He eventually returned to the University of Virginia, where he had conducted his residency in psychiatry.

For three decades, Dr. Greyson has focused his research on near-death experiences. He is a coauthor of *Irreducible Mind*, a massive work dedicated to modern psychology, and was the author of the overview of near-death experiences for the *Encyclopedia Britannica*. He has written more than one hundred articles in prestigious academic medical and psychological journals, including *The New England Journal of Medicine*, and has presented at more than eighty national and international scientific conferences.

He is the longtime editor of the *Journal of Near-Death Studies*. He is also cofounder and vice president of Cedar Creek Institute, whose mission is to explore areas of human potential neglected by contemporary science. The institute's research focuses on parapsychology experiences and behaviors.

Simply put, there is no one better I could have spoken with on the subject of near-death experiences. He is the foremost authority. I was extremely excited to meet him and talk with him.

Naturally I asked Jim to go with me, and we decided to make a road trip out of it, carting along Blue the Wonder Dog and his Frisbee. I took hours to pack a giant suitcase (even though I wore only about a third of whatever was in it) and a cooler full of yogurt, blueberries, carrots, and radishes. Jim, meanwhile, grabbed a minuscule duffel bag and packed in a nanosecond. I asked him what he wanted for the cooler. "Nothing," he replied. "I plan to live off the land." So while he gobbled down his double cheeseburger and fries at Burger King, I sat across from him with my dainty baggies of vegetables and fruit. This got old really fast. Luckily, we discovered the Cracker Barrel Restaurant, and I soon developed a love of trout, mashed potatoes, and green beans.

The only downside on our road trip was that we had to stay at pet-friendly hotels. Watching Blue sniff the outdated shag carpets for at least thirty minutes each time we checked in suggested that our room might not be as fresh and clean as we hoped. Driving cross-country from Idaho to Virginia on Interstate 80, we listened to Pat Conroy's *South of Broad* and Steve Martin's *An Object of Beauty*. We arrived at our destination safe and sound. Well, safe, anyway.

Charlottesville is nestled at the base of the Blue Ridge

Mountains and has a reputation as one of the most livable places in the country. It's rich with history. Three American presidents were raised in Charlottesville, and Thomas Jefferson founded the University of Virginia there in 1819. I was also pleased to learn that Charlottesville is a literary hub and has more newspaper readers per capita than anywhere else in America. My kind of town!

Cedar Creek Institute and the university's Division of Perceptual Studies occupy a building separate from the main campus. The offices also house the Ian Stevenson Memorial Library, one of only nine libraries in the world dedicated to parapsychological research. Use is restricted to scientists and qualified students and writers.

In Dr. Greyson's neatly appointed office, one wall is dominated by massive metal file cabinets filled with the many NDE cases he has studied. He was pleasant, gracious, and friendly. In his midsixties, he looks younger and is in great shape physically. He seemed a bit shy until he began talking about his work. His passion for it was obvious. I asked him what brought him to this field of study.

"I don't have a good answer for that," he said. "I grew up in a nonspiritual family of scientists. When I got to medical school, I gravitated to psychiatry because there were so many more unanswered questions there, such as the idea of people having hallucinations about the deceased. We used to think they happened only rarely. But then a family physician in England decided to just ask his patients if any of them had communication with a recently lost loved one. Amazingly, fifty percent said they had seen, heard, or smelled them. But if you do a study of the broader population, you won't get that level because people are reluctant to admit it."

I certainly understood that sentiment.

Dr. Greyson describes NDEs in *Irreducible Mind* and talked to us about them. "There is no universally agreed-on definition of NDEs, but they are generally understood to be the unusual, often vivid and realistic, and sometimes profoundly life-changing experiences occurring to people who have been either physiologically close to death, as in cardiac arrest or other life-threatening conditions, or psychologically close to death, as in accidents or illness in which they feared they would die." That makes sense.

He went on to explain that accounts of NDEs are numerous. They are also often underreported. At the University of Virginia alone, researchers have studied 861 reports. Studies in the last decade suggest that NDEs occur in about 10 to 20 percent of patients close to death. I was surprised and impressed by the frequency.

He talked about a book I'd never heard of but that is evidently well known within the field. It's called *Life After Life* and was written by physician and philosopher Raymond Moody, M.D., Ph.D., in 1975. Dr. Greyson told us that this book brought the existence of NDEs "out of the closet." It was based on more than 150 cases Dr. Moody had collected while he was working as an intern under Dr. Greyson. Dr. Moody cited a number of common characteristics of NDEs:

- A feeling of floating out of one's body and seeing it from a different perspective. Dr. Greyson has found this in 48 percent of NDEs.
- An awareness of what is going on, such as seeing doctors working on one.

- Moving through a long dark tunnel and sometimes meeting spirit guides or departed loved ones there. Dr. Greyson has found this in 42 percent of cases.
- Emerging from the tunnel to see a beautiful "Being of Light" that "speaks" to one, but nonverbally.
- Experiencing a life review or a revival of memories and receiving lessons or a judgment about how one lived one's life. Dr. Greyson has found this in 24 percent of NDEs.
- Seeing some other realm or border of great beauty where one cannot go.
- Experiencing intense joy and love.
- Returning to the body, often reluctantly.

We learned that other prominent researchers have confirmed Dr. Moody's characteristics of NDEs. Not every case has all these characteristics, and no single characteristic always occurs. Some NDEs have a completely different nature. NDE experiencers almost universally find it difficult to put into words what happened. I can understand why.

But, Dr. Greyson explains, a remarkable consistency to the accounts gives them credibility, and patients who have reported an NDE often cite astonishing things. They give specific, detailed accounts of what occurred in the operating room or their surroundings while they were "dead." They can recount unusual procedures or behavior they would otherwise have no way of knowing. And they can often quote the dialogue of the attending physicians and nurses.

One of the most dramatic accounts was documented by Dr. Greyson in a paper titled "Seeing Dead People Not Known to Have Died: 'Peak in Darien' Experiences," published in the journal *Anthropology and Humanism*. In the article Dr. Greyson cited patients whose NDEs included seeing, to their surprise, a person who had recently died—even though neither the patient nor anyone around the patient knew about the death at the time!

It's not just the NDEs themselves that are so remarkable. Other occurrences prior to death are surprising too.

"We've seen cases where people who have advanced Alzheimer's completely recover their lucidness days or hours before they die," Dr. Greyson said. "How can this be? The brain has physically deteriorated. But it happens, and there is no physiological explanation for this."

So how do we know that an NDE is not just a dream?

"One of the most striking things about NDEs is the way they totally transform people's lives. Those who have had NDEs nearly always say they are no longer afraid of dying," Dr. Greyson said. "Their lives are profoundly affected in other ways, even leading to such major changes as a career switch or divorce. As a psychiatrist, I deal with hallucinations all the time. They don't totally transform people's lives. Dreams don't either. But NDEs usually do, and that's why they are different."

"Could there be a medical explanation for NDEs?" I ask.

"There is currently no physiological explanation for near-death experiences, but that doesn't mean we will never find one," Dr. Greyson said.

Dr. Greyson acknowledges that NDEs fundamentally conflict with the conventional thinking that the brain creates consciousness. Instead, NDEs support the alternative view that the brain acts as a filter for consciousness, he said.

Despite the current scientific and medical views of the brain as the source of consciousness, the idea of the brain as a filter has been around for centuries, Dr. Greyson said.

"For example, there is considerable evidence that one mind can communicate with another—what we call telepathy. But there is no physiological explanation for that. If you think about it, it's no more puzzling than how does your mind make your hand write? We have no idea how that happens. Even if you accept the idea that the brain produces thoughts, which I don't, we can't explain how it happens. We haven't the slightest idea. Materialists say, 'Well, we will one day.' But that's not a scientific theory because it's not disprovable."

The best resource for research in this field is the patients themselves. But that presents scientists with some obstacles. First, doing research means "we have to wait for something to happen," Dr. Greyson said. "We can't orchestrate it. However, there are numerous documented cases going back to the ancient Greeks. And, of course, as we've seen from Dr. Eben Alexander, they are still happening today."

And, according to Dr. Greyson, research into NDEs will have to overcome another obstacle—people's reluctance to talk about them.

"I once conducted a study of people who had tried to commit suicide," Dr. Greyson said. "I interviewed them in a non-threatening way as soon as they had recovered. Some described leaving their body, but most told me that nothing unusual had happened. I followed up with them every month for over five years, and each year a few more would finally admit they did have an NDE but were previously afraid to talk about it. One person told me recently, twenty years later, that there were things he still wouldn't discuss with me because they are just too personal."

Public awareness of NDEs is changing that, Dr. Greyson said. "As bad as it still is, things are much better than they were in the eighties. At least now when I present at conferences, people are willing to discuss them in public," he said. "Even more encouraging is that medical students are getting excited about the field. I have two students upstairs right now doing research in our library."

I wanted Dr. Greyson's thoughts about what I had experienced since Max died. Did he think Max could be sending me messages through the handprints and other events?

"Looking at the photos, it's obvious that something out of the ordinary is happening," he said. "But the handprints, given their size, don't seem to have Max's signature, other than the timing of the anniversaries of his death. Is there a way you could ask him to get some more direction from him if this is really him? Perhaps your journey isn't over yet."

At the end of our conversation, Dr. Greyson said, "These things happening in your house—they may be coming from Max, and they may be coming from you. Maybe on the anniversaries you are filled with spirit and you somehow produce the effects. At a core level, perhaps there is no difference between you and Max—we're all part of the same thing. Maybe these barriers we put up between people are just temporary while we're here, and once you leave this body, it won't be like that."

I was deeply touched by this idea. Here we are, day in and day out, spending our lives as humans separated by the boundaries of our bodies. This naturally makes us think our minds and hearts are separate too. But what if they're not? What if we are, as Dr. Greyson suggests, part of the same consciousness and therefore inseparable? Is love the unifying factor that connects us to one another?

No other session throughout my journey touched me the way this particular conversation did. It was the only time I cried. Dr. Greyson had struck a deep chord inside me. As an M.D. and a professor, he had rooted the stunning phenomena, not in science, but in the most powerful experience we have in life—that of connectedness to one another.

CHAPTER 18

What's Worse Than Losing Your Spouse?

I had much to think about after the interview with Dr. Greyson. Not only had I learned that near-death experiences seemed to offer evidence of life beyond death, but I was reinforced in my belief that love extends across the boundaries between this life and the next. When it comes to our hearts, there is no difference between those we love here and those who are gone. I was also intrigued by the notion that the connection we feel when we love is fueled by something larger, something far more powerful than any one of us. As Dr. Greyson had put it, "We're all part of the same thing." I took this one step further in my own thinking. For me, this "thing" we're all a part of is love.

I started thinking about all the people I love. Jim and Tanner came to mind first and foremost, with a mental image of Maddie Hallerman, Tanner's longtime girlfriend, standing beside him. I visualized Michael and Ryan, Jim's sons, and Adriana,

Ryan's wife. I envisioned Kurt, Marky, Brian, Signe, and her husband, Dan, along with my nieces and nephews. I pictured Bob, Tanner's dad, whom I loved as the father of my son, and I immediately conjured up those Bob and Tanner loved in his family. I thought about my cherished women friends, some new, some old, all of whom had stood by me in good times and bad. I closed my eyes and saw their loved ones.

I couldn't help wondering how each of them would one day deal with the deaths of the people they loved. Depending on the extent of their relationship, would the loss change them in ways nothing else in their life had? Would they ask themselves what happens when we die? I wondered if they would encounter any of the types of phenomena I had experienced. Would they come to believe as I had that there is more beyond this world? Would that help them cope with their loss? And depending on who they lost, would the grief vary in magnitude just as the love does? Is all grief the same?

As sad as it is, we expect to bury our parents. But when the natural order is disturbed and a parent loses a child, it is the ultimate tragedy. There is no love like that of a parent for a child. It reigns supreme. As devastating as losing a spouse is, losing a child is worse. There can be no more crushing blow.

Ron and Lynn Dickerson know that. They lost their son Ryan at the age of eighteen in 2007 when he was found drowned in three feet of water at a summer camp where he was working. Authorities suspect that an undetected heart condition caused him to collapse.

Lynn is a friend of mine. She was the publisher of *The Modesto Bee* in California before becoming an executive in the corporate offices of the McClatchy Company. She's now back in Modesto as the CEO of the Gallo Center for the Arts. She's a smart, talented businesswoman and an accomplished leader who engenders loyalty and respect from her employees and colleagues.

She had been a devout Christian her whole life, but Ryan's death made her question her faith and sapped her will to live. Ryan was the younger of their two sons; Ross was twenty-two when Ryan died. Ryan was charming, fun, and caring and was loved by everyone.

"Seven weeks after Ryan died, I could barely get out of bed, brush my teeth, take a shower," Lynn told me. "For me it was the third year of my loss before I had color in my life again. When it's just happened, being told you'll be okay in two or three years is like being told in labor that it will go on for years. It doesn't seem survivable. To lose him has been almost unbearable. It's been almost six years, but we still carry this cloud of sadness around."

She pressed on because her husband and older son needed her. Very slowly, life became more tolerable. "It's like a leg being amputated. You can walk again with a prosthetic, but you'll always be an amputee," Lynn said.

Lynn could easily write her own book on her experiences of feeling connections or messages from Ryan. A friend's hairdresser who had psychic abilities said she could see Ryan and described him to the family friend. She even knew his idiosyncratic signature: rubbing his well-exercised abs and admiring himself in the mirror, a gesture that earned him constant teasing from his friends and family.

Ron met with the hairdresser immediately. She described their former house in Modesto and their new house in Sacramento. She knew that the kids jumped off a three-story balcony into the pool. She said Ryan was worried about them and two friends that she named.

Lynn's experience with the same psychic was less satisfying. Lynn was told she wasn't allowing herself to grieve. Although Lynn felt she had been misread, the medium did tell her that Ryan planned to leave coins to let them know he was with them. "Pennies can show up anywhere," Lynn said, but she has found them in the strangest places with connections to Ryan. She found one at her feet on a hiking trail in the Sierras with a grief support group. She found one on the ground as she was headed into a dinner with Hillary Clinton, Barack Obama, and John McCain during a newspaper conference. Ryan was a huge political junkie, and just as Lynn was wishing she could tell Ryan about the dinner, she saw the penny.

Lynn experienced flickering lights, much as I have. Every year family and friends hold a Christmas party called the Remembering Ryan Reunion, which helps ease Lynn's greatest fear—that Ryan will be forgotten. In the winter of 2009, Lynn had gathered up all her photos of Ryan and walked into the dining room to place them on the table. In the hallway, the fifteen canned lights all started going on and off like crazy. She yelled for Ron, and he rushed to the dining room. He began to cry, sensing that this was Ryan. She called Ross, her older son, who was highly skeptical of any paranormal events. They just stood there, amazed, until all the lights finally went off.

One of the most powerful events they experienced was a visit from Ryan's young friend and neighbor, who was very dis-approving of Lynn and Ron's talking to mediums and thought it was all nonsense. But he came to Lynn's door one day to tell her that Ryan had visited him during the night. The friend was awakened by his bed shaking, and there was Ryan at the foot of the bed, wearing a baseball jersey. Ryan was in a great place and was happy, he told his friend.

As the friend talked with Lynn and she referred to his "dream," he emphatically corrected her. It was *not* a dream; it was real, he said. His view had changed completely. The friend didn't understand why Ryan would visit him. Lynn's answer was, "Maybe he knew you needed him."

While Lynn read every book she could find on grief, her husband read every book he could find on after-death experiences and mediums. For Ron's Christmas gift, Lynn bought a personal telephone reading with George Anderson, the author of *Walking in the Garden of Souls*. They had a neighbor arrange the reading and use his credit card so that the medium could not research the Dickersons ahead of time. Lynn listened on another phone line during the reading.

Anderson said he saw two boys, Ron's son (Ryan) and Ron's brother. Ron had lost his eighteen-year-old brother thirty-eight years earlier. Anderson said the boys seemed to be good friends and were linking pinkies together. He said Ryan also was with Lynn's deceased sister. (Lynn's mother had a stillborn daughter when Lynn was in the sixth grade.)

Anderson said Ryan was very happy about how he was being remembered, and he especially liked the "planting." (Lynn and Ron dedicated a steel art oak tree sculpture to the public library in Ryan's name.) Anderson knew the Dickersons were moving soon. He said their other son had been somewhat difficult growing up (true) and asked if someone named Sarah was important. (Their fourteen-year-old dog, named Sarah, grew up with Ryan and died just months before him.)

Nothing about any of these events scared them, Lynn said. On the contrary, they were comforting and helped ease their grief. "I felt like it was a gift," Lynn said. "I felt like I was holding on to life by a thread, and it gave me a new hold."

Lynn has reached out to many grieving parents and always asks them if they have received signs from their children. Only one woman, a committed atheist, has said no.

Bob and Phran Ginsberg also had to deal with the tragedy of losing a child. I met them at the annual meeting of the Forever Family Foundation where I had met Loyd Auerbach and Dr. Eben Alexander. Bob and Phran are the founders of the organization. It was their own personal loss and the journey that followed that led them to establish it.

Bob said that before the loss of their child, "I didn't believe in psychic phenomena, and I didn't believe in survival [after death] simply because my left-brain thinking just couldn't imagine these things as being real. My background is not in science. I have a B.A. in English from the State University of New York, did a little bit of graduate work, and got into the insurance business."

Phran, on the other hand, had psychic experiences throughout her life. Even as a child, she would know things she couldn't explain, and she had premonitions. Fortunately, they were always positive. But on September 1, 2002, Phran woke up Bob between three and four a.m. with her first negative premonition.

"She was ashen white and trembling," Bob said. "I said, 'What's the matter?' She said, 'I don't know, but something horrible is going to happen today.' So I said, 'Well, what?' and she said, 'I can't put my finger on it, but I know it's something horrible.'

"Ordinarily I would dismiss something like that," Bob said. But he knew Phran's precognition had proven accurate in the past, so he took her concern seriously. Their first thought was their children. "We watched over our children throughout the day," Bob said. "My middle daughter [Kori] had just started college at Carnegie Mellon. We had the car packed up to take my son [Jonathan] back to the University of Delaware the next day, and my youngest daughter, Bailey, was working the last day of her summer job before returning to high school. We checked on all three during the day but let our guard down at the end of the day."

They were driving home from a restaurant in two cars, with Jonathan driving the first car and Bailey as his passenger. "My son and daughter were in a horrible accident, and we came upon the scene minutes after the crash," Bob said. "He was seriously injured, and she didn't survive.

"You can imagine the shock. For a while I didn't know if I was going to lose two children. Eventually my son recovered, and it was about that time that it hit me like a ton of bricks. 'Wait a second, how did Phran know?' I knew Phran would never lie to me, so I knew that her so-called paranormal experiences were real, but I needed some verification from a scientific point of view that such things were possible.

"My search was not an altruistic endeavor to help people in the beginning. It was a matter of my own survival because, quite frankly, I was such a mess. I didn't really see any way I could personally survive the loss. I mean, it was utterly devastating. I read, which I still do to this day, literally hundreds and hundreds of books on the topic of survival, the theory that some part of us continues after we die."

Phran believes Bailey reached out to the Ginsbergs from the other side in many ways, but the most dramatic came on the first Christmas morning after the September accident. Jonathan was recovering and was at his girlfriend's house. Kori was home from college for the holidays. Bob, Phran, and Kori could not bring themselves to celebrate Christmas Eve in their normal way with friends, so they went to bed early. Sleep was often an escape from their grief.

"Kori came running into our room, crying hysterically," Phran said. Bailey had appeared to Kori and asked her to tell Bailey's friends they shouldn't freak out if Bailey visited them, Kori said. Bob and Phran invited Kori to climb into bed with them, but at eighteen, she preferred to sleep on the floor at the foot of their bed.

After the lights were off, Phran felt one of their cats jump on the bed. She sat up and saw that Kori had moved up onto the bed, so she warned Bob not to kick her, and they went to sleep. In the morning, Phran found Kori on the floor and asked her why she had moved back down. Kori told her she had never moved up onto the bed. Bailey and Kori were only two years apart, and Phran is sure that it was Bailey sleeping with them on that Christmas morning. "This was her way of saying, 'I'm okay,'" Phran said.

Phran said Bob had dreams in which he and Bailey talked, but he wasn't having the kinds of experiences she and Kori were having. "Kori and I found comfort in these signs, but Bob was going deeper and deeper into grief," Phran said. "He was on a science mission to figure this thing out."

Bob couldn't understand why a warning sign would come to someone if there was not enough information to prevent the tragedy. He was working with a grief counselor, and so was the family. They were trying to attend a Compassionate Friends support group, but they kept missing the monthly meeting times by a day or two.

One afternoon, Phran was on her way to pick up Jonathan from physical rehab when her mind could not stop focusing on a strange question. A young girl named Deanna Moon had died in an accident years ago at the elementary school that Phran's children attended, and Phran was suddenly consumed with knowing how old Deanna would be if she had lived. She had no idea why she wanted to know. Jonathan couldn't tell her the answer. When they got home, Bob hustled them into the car for a meeting of Compassionate Friends an hour away. One of the participants turned out to be Deanna Moon's mother, and the Ginsbergs learned that Deanna, who died at age nine, would have been celebrating her twenty-first birthday that day. This event helped convince Bob that communications from the afterlife had a purpose beyond warnings.

As the Ginsbergs met other people with similar experiences, they quickly found a broad reluctance to talk openly. The moderator from one group shut them down if they brought up the afterlife.

"In his view, that was not the purpose of the group," Bob said. "The purpose of the group was teaching methods people could utilize to deal with their grief. We thought this to be odd, since belief in the afterlife is perhaps the most effective form of grief therapy. It didn't take long to find that other parents wanted to discuss the possibility that their children still survived, so we stood out in parking lots, sometimes shivering our butts off in the cold. We would talk for hours. We finally concluded that we needed to form some sort of organization where we could discuss these things openly, without fear of being labeled."

They happened upon a book called *The Afterlife Experiments* by Dr. Gary Schwartz, the professor I had met at Canyon Ranch, and it led to a friendship with him and the formation of Forever Family Foundation in 2004. The goal was to merge science and spirituality, support research into the evidence of survival after death, educate the public, and help the bereaved. *How gratifying to know this is out there for bereaved parents*, I thought, a true support group to help others navigate this nearly impossible task of overcoming the grief from the death of one's child.

"We don't preach to anybody, and we don't try to convince anybody," Bob said. "We simply want to make known the evidence that exists. When it comes to a belief in an afterlife, people will always move at their own pace. Some will never be open to it. I see the effect that grief has, and often there is a progression as they move from hope to belief and eventually to a knowing. Once they get to that knowing stage, it can make a significant difference in their lives."

Phran added, "The whole momentum that drove the creation of this organization is that everybody thinks we're nuts, and we're not. If we put everybody in a room, we'd be the majority."

Bob stressed the importance of research into survival of consciousness by such scientists as Dr. Dean Radin and Dr. Bruce Greyson. Some people ask why research on telepathy or precognition is relevant to the afterlife, Bob said. "Once people learn that your mind can act independently of your brain, as it does with things like remote viewing and telepathy, then it's a logical step to conclude that your consciousness can survive physical death—that it can survive without a brain. You have to back into it with a lot of people," Bob said.

Interestingly, their organization encourages the use of mediums, primarily as a way for people to learn whether departed loved ones are safe and happy. This was something I wanted to learn more about, as I'd had no experience with mediums at this point in my journey. If anything, I was skeptical of mediums.

But I was impressed to learn that Forever Family Foundation has developed what the Ginsbergs believe is the only protocol to certify a medium as credible, other than in scientific research programs.

I wanted to know what advice the Ginsbergs and Lynn would give to grieving parents—or anyone else.

Lynn said she tells people all the time to recognize that losing a child is a loss different from any other. "We had lost parents or friends. But they were all like a trip to Disneyland compared to losing our son," she said. "You can't even imagine the depth of the pain you suffer. But you just have to feel the pain. There's no avoiding it. It hurts like hell for a very long time."

The most important thing friends and family can do is let the bereaved person talk about it, Lynn said. "We want to hear our child's name said again. Don't try to hush us or change the subject because it's uncomfortable. Let us tell our story," she said. Lynn said it infuriated her when people told her they couldn't survive such a loss, "like they thought I could. What is my choice?"

Bereaved parents need a friend who will sit with them in their sadness. "People disappear because they don't know what to say or will say the wrong thing. For me, people pretending nothing had happened was hurtful to me." She also tells other parents, "Just know that you won't always hurt this badly forever. You will get to the point that you can smile again, and laugh again."

Bob said, "I used to say to myself, 'If I can only make it through the first year, I'll be okay.' But then the first year went by, and I really wasn't okay. My advice would be to learn, share, and remain open not only to one's own personal experiences, but also to the experiences of others. When people open up to the possibilities, sometimes their world can change with the information they learn.

"It doesn't mean you're not going to fall back into despair. I used to hate it when people would say to me, 'Time heals all wounds.' It infuriated me. But it's true that as time goes by, it gets different. It's not that your grief will ever disappear. You will always have a hole in your heart. But it does get different. And in many cases that difference is the result of remaining open and sharing. That's the key."

CHAPTER 19

Mediums: Real or Fiction?

Having been introduced to the concept of mediums by Bob and Phran, I was curious. What is a medium anyway? When we visited Dr. Greyson at the University of Virginia, he had taken us on a tour of the Ian Stevenson Memorial Library and given me some articles that were helpful.

A medium is someone who "claim[s] to communicate information about deceased persons that the medium had no normal way of knowing," according to Dr. Emily Kelly of the Department of Perceptual Studies at the University of Virginia in a 2011 article in *The Journal of Nervous and Mental Disease*. This is different from psychics, who "give their clients or 'sitters,' primary information about the sitters themselves or other living persons," Dr. Kelly writes. In other words, it seems to me a medium is having a conversation, and a psychic is observing.

Dr. Gary Schwartz and his team at the University of Arizona conducted some of the first laboratory experiments in the United States using mediums. I wanted to talk with him in more detail and decided to travel yet again. This time I went alone. I flew to Tucson and met with Dr. Schwartz at his office. It wasn't as much fun without Jim and Blue, but at least no one complained about how heavy my suitcase was or made comments about my rabbit food.

In addition to his role at Canyon Ranch, Dr. Schwartz is a professor of psychology, medicine, neurology, psychiatry, and surgery at the University of Arizona in Tucson. He received his Ph.D. in psychology from Harvard University and was an assistant professor at Harvard for five years. He later served as a professor of psychology and psychiatry at Yale University and was director of the Yale Psychophysiology Center and codirector of the Yale Behavior Medicine Service. Among other books, he wrote *The Truth About Medium* (including the real Allison DuBois, the inspiration for the TV show *Medium*) and *The G.O.D. Experiments*. Recently, Dr. Schwartz has been named chairman of Eternea, an organization founded by *Proof of Heaven* author Dr. Eben Alexander.

In the experiments conducted at the University of Arizona, Dr. Schwartz took great care to choose mediums with a record of accuracy and to control for potential cheating and fraud. The team found that, as a group, the mediums were accurate 83 percent of the time in producing information about deceased relatives. One medium achieved 93 percent accuracy.

That, of course, doesn't mean that every person who claims to be a medium has that ability or that every medium's reading is a conversation with a spirit. Dr. Greyson told me, "When you talk to someone who has been to a medium and had a positive experience, it's not necessarily because facts came through that satisfied them. It's often because they say they could feel the personality."

But the evidence can't be easily brushed away, Dr. Greyson said. "Here at the University of Virginia we did some controlled studies like Gary Schwartz's," Dr. Greyson said. "We made sure that the sitters and the mediums were never in the same place, and we got results similar to Gary's with six mediums. In fact, one of the mediums was almost always correct." This same medium happened to be the most accurate of the mediums Dr. Schwartz had tested in his research.

Dr. Schwartz told me that his and other scientific experiments suggest that consciousness lives on after we die—and takes a form that has intention and will. So he, like Dr. Wendland, Dr. Radin, and Dr. Greyson, believes consciousness is more than a product of our brains—it lives outside of us and continues after we die. I learned he believes that "spirit," a term he uses for consciousness after death, collaborates with us in our daily lives and asserts itself creatively and convincingly, if we pay attention.

Dr. Schwartz's prominence in this field led to an invitation to write an influential chapter in *The Oxford Handbook of Psychology and Spirituality*. The chapter is titled "Consciousness, Spirituality and Post-Materialist Science: An Empirical and Experiential Approach."

Dr. Schwartz gave me a copy of the chapter. He writes quite convincingly that the current scientific assumption that consciousness ends when the body dies is just plain wrong. Reading the piece, I was reminded of his considerable skill at analogy, which I had seen him display in his class at Canyon Ranch.

Dr. Schwartz argues that the brain is like a television. TVs are not the source of visual information but rather detect and display it. In the same way, he says, the brain is a receiver, not a creator, an argument similar to those of others with whom I spoke on my journey. And this, of course, implies that the death of the brain does not cut off the source of information. I use this analogy over and over in my mind as a way to assimilate the information at a basic level and make sense of it.

Another of my favorite analogies I learned from Dr. Schwartz involves a fan. Imagine facing a fan before it is turned on. You can clearly see the blades, but you cannot see what is behind the blades. The blades block that view. But when you impart energy to the fan by turning it on, you can no longer see the blades, even though you can see everything behind the fan.

"Is it possible that could be a metaphor for the spirit world?" Dr. Schwartz said. "We can't see the spirits [blades] because they operate at a higher energy level. But they clearly are there."

I had this in mind after Jim and I returned from our annual anniversary trip to his ranch on the Middle Fork of the Salmon River. I had recently taken up photography and had purchased a new digital camera. On the return trip in the tiny Cessna plane, I was taking pictures of the stunning vista of the Frank Church–River of No Return Wilderness Area below us.

When I got home, I was looking at some of the pictures showing the view out of the front of the plane. To my eye when I took these pictures, they were unobstructed shots. But with the aid of the rapid light capture of the camera, several pictures recorded images of the plane's propeller. Because of the propeller's speed, I couldn't see it. But the camera confirmed that it was there all along. It crystallized the concept that just because we can't see something with our eyes, it doesn't mean it's not there.

As I had learned at Canyon Ranch, Dr. Schwartz has dedicated his career to trying to determine whether spirits from the afterlife—or elsewhere—exist. He wrote about one experiment in an article titled "Possible Application of Silicon Photomultiplier Technology to Detect the Presence of Spirit and Intention: Three Proof-of-Concept Experiments" in the May–June 2010 edition of the journal *Explore*. This article was definitely challenging for those of us who are not scientifically inclined or trained. I had to spend a lot of time going over it, but I was intent upon grasping what I could. Eventually, it made sense to me.

In his experiment, Dr. Schwartz used a miniature, highly sensitive device that detects photons, which are particles of light. The device was placed in a tightly controlled black plastic box designed to eliminate all outside light. The experimenter then invited "spirit" to enter the box. The results in each of the three experiments showed a measurable increase in photons in the box after spirit was invited.

Some scientists, including Dr. Schwartz, questioned whether the experimenter himself might be causing the results because, as I had learned, quantum physics suggests the observer affects—and probably determines—measurements. So Dr. Schwartz conducted two follow-up experiments. They were described in another article in *Explore* in its March–April 2011 edition titled "Photonic Measurement of Apparent Presence of Spirit Using a Computer Automated System." These experiments also used a highly sensitive photon-detecting, low-light camera in a light-tight room. (How's that for a layperson explanation?) But this time a computer, using both visual and auditory information, gave all the instructions to spirit without the experimenters' presence or awareness. The results indicated that the experimenter's presence could not explain the increases in patterns of light after spirit was invited to enter.

In the piece I had read earlier by Dr. Emily Kelly from the University of Virginia, she warned of the risks of using a medium. It's important to evaluate whether information from a medium could have come from another source, Dr. Kelly wrote.

"One common normal explanation for mediumship is that the medium fishes for information ("cold reading"), whether deliberately or inadvertently, by first making vague or general statements and then taking any feedback or clues from the sitter's responses or appearance to further refine and focus those vague statements," Dr. Kelly wrote. "Even when the medium does not allow the sitter to say anything but 'yes' or 'no' in response to a statement, he or she can nonetheless obtain a great deal of information and direction from such replies."

I discussed the topic of mediums briefly with Dr. Radin when Jim and I visited him in Petaluma. His view is that scientifically legitimate evidence indicates that talented mediums can get confirmable information by nonordinary means. But he added that the evidence is not clear on whether the information came from a deceased person.

"The interpretation of experiments on mediumship is not settled, and there is no easy resolution in sight," Dr. Radin told me. "In general, people should always be skeptical of what mediums say, but not so skeptical that they can no longer hear what is being said; i.e., be skeptical and open at the same time. This is not always easy to accomplish if there is strong emotion wrapped into the purpose of a reading, so it is useful to be accompanied by someone who does not have an emotional reason to believe what the medium is saying."

I came to the conclusion that it was time for me to get firsthand experience. I wanted to try it myself.

I arranged a session with Dave Campbell, a medium who is certified by Forever Family Foundation. With Dave's approval I recorded the session. Remembering what Dr. Radin had said, I asked Dave if Jim could be there. Dave was fine with that.

Dave is a very amicable man in his late thirties or early forties. He was friendly and professional in his demeanor, and I was completely comfortable around him. He was very "normal" and not at all intimidating. He suggested we sit in chairs across from each other. Jim sat at a distance behind us at a desk so as not to interfere.

Dave started, "The way it works is spirit talks to me. I hear words. I feel emotions. I just describe what they are showing me. It has no meaning to me. I just pass on what they say."

Over the next fifty minutes, Dave shared with us the messages he said the spirit world was communicating to him. He did not know Max's name or that I was trying to communicate with Max. We had told him nothing, literally nothing.

While he mentioned a few other names that weren't relevant in the beginning, halfway through he suddenly said, "I see an M." He then said this "M" spirit "wishes you joy and happiness and wants you to go forward in your life. He says he helped arrange things. Connect the dots. I feel like he was very protective and very helpful. He is watching over you from the other side."

Does this mean that Max had "arranged" the hand on the mirror, the moving rugs, the footprint, and other events? And the part about feeling protective and watching over me from the other side was comforting but very generic. I was not sure what to think.

As the session proceeded, Jim and I both felt that the

accuracy was mixed. We weren't talking to each other, but we were sharing eye contact and body language. Some of the things we heard were simply wrong. Others were just confusing. For example, a meaningful part of the communication seemed to be directed to Jim and involved his father.

We did, however, experience a surprising introduction to an issue that can arise when working with mediums. A medium will often ask the person sitting for the reading to continue to think about the messages long after the session is over. It is apparently common for a sitter to recognize a connection or meaning later. This is exactly what happened to Jim and me. Dave asked a very specific question that had nothing to do with Max and made absolutely no sense to either of us. In fact, it was such an odd and obscure question, we talked about it after we left and wondered how Dave had gone so far afield.

But about a year later, this very question was answered in such a way that we were stunned by the legitimacy of Dave's insight. It had to do with a medical issue that Jim prefers to keep private. Simply put, Dave had predicted the future. He went beyond his capacity as a medium. He was psychic, as well. His accuracy and specificity were ultimately chilling.

There was one more truly amazing aspect of this reading. At the very end, Dave was quiet for a minute or two and then looked up and said, "I think that's all I'm getting. I hope you found it useful. Do you have any questions?"

I didn't really feel the need for more questions. But Jim spoke up and said, "Dave, just one more thing. Do you see anything that has to do with hands? From M...Max, I mean."

Now, this is narrowing the scope a little bit, to be sure. But there is still a wide range of possibilities. It could be the reading of hands, like palmistry, or praying hands, maybe holding hands, perhaps a sculpture of hands. So it was, I think, a fair question.

Dave said nothing for quite a while and remained perfectly still in his chair. I was starting to get a little antsy, when suddenly he spoke up and said, "I see handprints. Like on a window or a mirror."

CHAPTER 20

Challenging the Scientific Community

Research by Dr. Radin and others suggests that humans have telepathic ability. Scientifically controlled experiments have measured it. Of course, individual abilities vary, just as they do in sports, music, or art. Yet mainstream scientists, for the most part, refuse to accept evidence of psi phenomena or choose to ignore it. They are skeptical. I respect and understand skepticism. We in the newspaper industry are trained skeptics. Reporters repeatedly question the validity or truth of what they are told by a source. Certainly scientists do the same. It's what they're supposed to do.

When I mentioned to Dr. Bruce Greyson that I was skeptical about mediums, his response was what I would expect it to be. He said, "I'm skeptical about everything."

But when healthy questioning morphs into a refusal to consider new information, it becomes bias. As Loyd Auerbach put it, "How is it scientific to ignore these things? It's the most unscientific thing they could do."

To help me understand the paradox of scientific resistance to parapsychology as a discipline and put my own experiences into a greater context, I asked Dr. Radin to recommend a resource. He referred me to Dr. Charles Tart, a commanding figure in the world of parapsychology. He said Dr. Tart understood after-death communications like the ones I was having as well as anyone he knew in the field.

I contacted Dr. Tart, and he was more than amenable to getting together. This meant, yes, another road trip! Jim, Blue, and I drove over from Sun Valley to California in just two days. (I packed a smaller giant bag, Jim took his Dopp kit, and Blue took his trusted Frisbee.)

Breaking up our travel time, we spent the night in Jackpot, Nevada, at the fabled Cactus Pete's Resort Casino. Walking through the casino to our room, I could hear the ubiquitous sounds of slot machines in the background, sounding almost like a carnival. The casino's grand public rooms were in stark contrast to nature's humble desert just outside the front door. We slept well, had a hearty breakfast the next morning in the casino cafe (well, Jim's pancakes were hearty, my yogurt not so much), and headed out to California.

We arrived at Dr. Tart's home, tucked in the hills near the University of California, Berkeley, on a spectacularly beautiful and sunny day. It was tricky maneuvering our rather bulky Toyota Sequoia SUV through the narrow roads.

Dr. Tart greeted Jim and me at the front door of his charming home with a broad smile and a hearty handshake. He led us to his office in a separate cottage on the property among the thick trees. He could not have been more gracious. Following behind him, I noticed he was very tall and probably in his midseventies. He was dressed casually and wore large framed glasses. Entering his office, I could see that it was more than an office. This was an intimate sanctuary, filled with the life of Charles Tart. Photos of family, professional associates, and trips taken, floor-to-ceiling shelves crowded with books that had clearly been read and referenced many times over. Dr. Tart sat at his large desk in a comfortable chair that looked worn in the right way, hands folded, while we sat on the couch across from him. As busy as he is, he had not only found the time for us, but he was present in his time with us. No distractions, no preoccupations. He was a gentleman.

Dr. Tart has been at the forefront of the study of parapsychology for at least five decades. His contributions have been instrumental in the public's gradual but growing awareness on the subject. Among the field's scientists I interviewed, it was clear that "Charley," as his colleagues call him, is loved and respected by all.

As usual, I asked him to tell me his own story.

Dr. Tart studied electrical engineering at the Massachusetts Institute of Technology, but he soon realized that his true calling was psychology. So he transferred first to Duke University, the home of J. B. Rhine's world-famous parapsychology lab. Then he moved a few miles away to the University of North Carolina, where he earned a bachelor's degree, master's degree, and Ph.D. in psychology.

He received postdoctoral training in hypnosis research at Stanford University. He is professor emeritus of psychology at the University of California, Davis, where he served on the faculty for twenty-eight years. He also is an executive faculty member at the Institute of Transpersonal Psychology, now called Sofia University, and serves on the advisory board of the Rhine Research Center.

Dr. Tart has authored or coauthored fourteen books. He wants his books to be read by everyone, not just the scientific community. He joked with us, "I only write books for people who are going to die." His writing style is so accessible that it once cost him an academic promotion he wanted and deserved. He was told his books were so clearly written that they couldn't possibly be of academic quality.

I asked him to talk about after-death communications (ADCs) and told him briefly about my experiences. His response to the handprints on the mirror was consistent with Dr. Radin's. He wasn't surprised by them.

We talked about his book *The End of Materialism*, in which he cites work by Bill and Judy Guggenheim in which they documented the types and characteristics of after-death communications in the late 1980s. Based on interviews with more than two thousand people, they found that experiencers of ADCs reported sensing a presence, hearing a voice, feeling a touch, or smelling a fragrance. They also included visions (from transparent to full, solid reality), telephone calls, paranormal movement of objects, and various signs from the deceased. There were reported cases of out-of-body experiences and sleep-state experiences where reality is altered as a person is either falling asleep or coming awake. Sometimes these are reported not as dreams but as vivid experiences of contact with the deceased. Finally, there were also cases of altered states in which communication is experienced through meditation or prayer.

Listening to Dr. Tart describe this research reinforced what I now realized: that much of what I had experienced had been experienced by others. When I had my out-of-body experience,

I thought it was unusual because I knew nothing about it and had never experienced anything remotely like it. But after I visited the Monroe Institute in Virginia, I learned I wasn't the first person to have this happen. Until I met Dr. Wendland in Ventura, Dr. Radin in Petaluma, Dr. Schwartz in Tucson, and Dr. Greyson in Charlottesville, I knew nothing about the research on consciousness. Now I knew there was a body of work supporting the premise that consciousness survives death.

I had enormous respect and appreciation for these men who cut against the grain of their traditional academic and scientific universes to risk the stigma of the field of parapsychology. When anyone draws outside the lines of a discipline, they have to have courage. There wasn't one professional I had met so far on my journey who had thin skin. These people weren't taking the easy path of endorsement and reinforcement. They were taking the hard path of following what they believed to be worthwhile, despite the ridicule and skepticism.

As I showed Dr. Tart my photos, he quickly, but very kindly, suggested a number of things I should have done, like taking fingerprints off the mirror or getting a sample of the material from the handprints for forensic analysis. Then he looked up at my face and apologized.

"I'm a nerd, you understand," he said with a twinkle in his eyes.

"Yes, I know I should have. But at the time, I only thought to take a photo. I'm not a scientist, you understand." And we both laughed.

I wanted him to talk about the resistance by mainstream scientists to the study of parapsychology. I had brought along *The End of Materialism* in my backpack and pulled it out. This is a book written by a very smart academic, yet I not only read it front to back, but relished it. There was a reason. Dr. Tart's writing style made it possible. I was happy to open it up in his presence with a bit of drama and show him all my notes and underlining.

In his book, Dr. Tart describes materialism as the view that the vast majority of scientists accept. It is the assumption that electrical currents and chemical reactions of the brain are what create consciousness. Said another way, no brain, no consciousness. Naturally, this precludes consciousness surviving death and made the events I had experienced impossible.

But Dr. Tart's view is that these materialists are disregarding the facts. He notes that people throughout the world and throughout history have reported psi activities. And what constitutes psi activity, according to Dr. Tart? He defines the "big five" of psi as telepathy, clairvoyance, precognition, psychokinesis, and psychic healing.

"Each of the big five has hundreds of well-controlled experiments supporting its existence as well as hundreds of thousands of events reportedly happening to ordinary people in everyday life that are most likely caused by these psi functions," he said. Those who discount this evidence are not only ignoring it, but, worse, are practicing science improperly, Dr. Tart contends.

In his book, he cited the view of Abraham Maslow, a founder of humanistic psychology: "Used correctly, science can be an open-ended, error-correcting, personal growth system of great power. Used incorrectly and inappropriately, science can be one of the best and most prestigious neurotic defense mechanisms available." As Maslow put it, "Science, then, can be a defense. It can be primarily a safety philosophy, a security system, a complicated way of avoiding anxiety and upsetting problems."

Dr. Tart calls this predicament "scientism."

"Scientism in our time consists mainly of a dogmatic commitment to a materialistic philosophy that dismisses and explains away the spiritual, rather than actually examining it carefully and trying to understand it," Dr. Tart said. Even worse is when that refusal to examine spiritual phenomena is wrapped in the mantle of science, he said. He sees this as "a perversion of genuine science."

"Being a skeptic," he said, "is a rational and sensible strategy in life. There are a lot of things we think we know that we may well be mistaken about. Being a skeptic is also an honorable, high-status social role, especially in intellectual circles. We tend to think of skeptics as smarter and sharper than those who just unquestioningly accept whatever they're told. Being a skeptic implies being a smart person who has looked more closely than most usually do and has investigated something more thoroughly, because he or she wants to know the truth, or at least a better approximation to the truth, about these things."

And then there's what he calls "pseudoskeptics." They claim to be skeptics, interested in getting at the truth while doubting the adequacy of current explanations. They actually adhere to and advocate some other belief system that, they believe, already has all the necessary truth. This adds confusion to the legitimate skeptical questions being asked, Dr. Tart said.

The various practitioners I interviewed offer their findings and experiences as "evidence" that consciousness survives physical death. That's very different from claiming "proof." Proof has been elusive. But there is sufficient evidence that is consistent, has been replicated under scientific controls, and is recurring with enough frequency that it shouldn't be ignored.

When I met with Dr. Radin, he put it this way: "The

question is not whether there is any scientific evidence, but rather what does an evaluation of the evidence reveal?" In other words, Dr. Radin said, "critical thinking is a double-edged sword: it must be applied to any claim, including the claims of skeptics." I could not agree more.

In Dr. Radin's book *The Conscious Universe*, he states,

> The tendency to adopt a fixed set of beliefs and defend them to the death is incompatible with science, which is essentially a loose confederation of evolving theories in many domains. Unfortunately, this tendency has driven some scientists to continue to defend outmoded, inaccurate worldviews. The tendency is also seen in the behavior of belligerent skeptics who loudly proclaim that widespread belief in psi reflects a decline in the public's critical thinking ability. One hopes that such skeptics would occasionally apply a little skepticism to their own positions, but history amply demonstrates that science advances mainly by funerals, not by reason and logic alone.

He reminded me that Copernicus and Galileo were publicly humiliated and socially rejected for their views. And in those days failure to toe the line of accepted theories could be life threatening. At least now it's not a life-or-death proposition. But it still carries the prospect of public humiliation and ridicule and, in the academic community, a threat to a scientific career. I got a smile from the 1996 headline on a *New York Times Magazine* article about Dr. Radin that said, THEY LAUGHED AT GALILEO TOO.

Just because a theory is scoffed at initially doesn't mean it's wrong. Only controlled scientific research will determine a theory's value. Skeptics aren't going away, but neither are the scientists and researchers who want to understand consciousness.

So what will it take to remove the stigma of talking about after-death communications and psi phenomena and move us forward? I asked Dr. Tart why the documented successes of parapsychology have been so little recognized.

"Remember that scientific parapsychology is a very small-scale enterprise, and it's taken decades to collect this evidence," Dr. Tart said. "My current rough estimate is that only a few dozen people are conducting parapsychological research, and that's on a strictly part-time basis. I doubt that the total worldwide parapsychological research in a year would equal an hour of any mainstream field's research."

Then there's the funding shortage that generally plagues this field. Dr. Tart likened it to the curing of the common cold. "It's as if the grants are given by saying, 'Let's cure the common cold. Here's thirteen thousand dollars a year to cure the common cold,'" he said. "Well, it's a little more complicated than that."

Perhaps the greatest challenge is creating a controlled environment for research. Dr. Tart uses the analogy of electricity.

"We first knew about electricity because lightning strikes," he said. "But it strikes, and then it's over. It's hard to learn anything when it's over. We run our shoes across a rug and sometimes get a spark of static electricity, so we know about that. But then it's over. The fact is we didn't know anything about electricity until we got a battery. The battery created electricity that was steady, reliable, and stronger than intermittent static sparks. If parapsychology could create the equivalent of a battery, then we could really begin to understand. But until then we have to deal with spontaneous cases like NDEs or the events you experienced. They happen, and then they're gone."

If, as Dr. Radin argues, public demand will produce more research, are there signs that public sentiment is changing?

Certainly there are signs of that. A recent phenomenon has emerged to focus the attention of everyday people on questions surrounding death. News stories in the summer of 2013 described something called Death Cafes, a type of gathering that had sprung up in nearly forty cities in the last year. They aren't grief support groups or planning sessions for end-of-life concerns. They are generally monthly meetings where interested people talk about what death is like, why we fear it, and how our perceptions of death affect how we live. Participants also discuss what the afterlife might be like and share stories of dreams or "visits" from loved ones who have died. The cafes, patterned after similar European salons, are opening up what has tended to be a taboo subject for Americans.

A recent article in *The Wall Street Journal* focused on a class offered by Dr. Norma Bowe at Kean University titled "Death in Perspective." It has a three-year waiting list. The article states that there are thousands of courses on dying and mortality being taught at college campuses nationwide.

Scientific skeptics also may be shifting their views in small ways, Dr. Radin said. "In recent years, the few skeptics who have studied the scientific evidence in detail have significantly moderated their previous opinions, but this has not been well publicized," he said.

After *Newsweek* magazine ran a cover story on Dr. Eben Alexander's book, despite the swift criticism from Sam Harris, the noted atheist and cognitive neuroscientist, Dr. Harris included an opening for seeing consciousness as separate from the brain.

"As many of you know, I am interested in 'spiritual' experiences of the sort Alexander reports," Dr. Harris wrote in his blog. "Unlike many atheists, I don't doubt the *subjective* phenomena themselves—that is, I don't believe that everyone who claims to have seen an angel, or left his body in a trance, or become one with the universe, is lying or mentally ill. And, unlike many neuroscientists and philosophers, I remain agnostic on the question of how consciousness is related to the physical world."

I asked Dr. Radin why there is so much myth versus truth about psi phenomena.

"Skeptics who have attempted to block psi research through the use of rhetoric and ridicule have also been responsible for perpetuating the many popular myths associated with psychic phenomena," he explained. "If serious scientists are prevented from investigating claims of psi out of fear for their reputations, then who is left to conduct these investigations? Extreme skeptics? No, because the fact is that most extremists do not conduct research; they specialize in criticism. Extreme believers? No, because they are usually not interested in conduction of rigorous scientific studies."

What about offering a public challenge?

In February 2013, a group of Internet leaders including Yuri Milner, a Russian entrepreneur; Sergey Brin, a cofounder of Google; Mark Zuckerberg, the founder of Facebook; and Anne Wojcicki, founder of the genetics company 23andMe, established a new award called the Breakthrough Prize in Life Sciences. According to a *New York Times* article published February 20, 2013, Ms. Wojcicki said the prize "was meant to reward scientists who think big, take risks, and have made a significant impact on our lives." According to the article, each scientist named will receive the "world's richest academic prize for medicine and biology—$3 million each, more than twice the amount of the Nobel Prize."

Why not fund the study of consciousness? Serious awards for serious scientists investigating consciousness to prove or disprove that it exists separately from brain function would be incredibly worthwhile. Maybe the leaders in the high-tech or entertainment industries might be open to it. They reside in innovative, risk-taking businesses that require imagination. They excel at inventing. This would be a chance to do just that. With funding, awareness would rise, and with heightened awareness, anything is possible.

An analogy I've often given when discussing this topic of funding research during my interviews with the various scientists is the Susan G. Komen organization. The organization was conceived in 1982 to fight breast cancer and has successfully raised awareness and funding, most notably through the signature Race for the Cure. According to their website, they have invested more than $2.5 billion in research and programs. They started with $200 and "a shoebox full of potential donor names" and over time have become the largest breast cancer organization in the United States. Awareness changed everything as women came forward. Funding, which had been focused primarily on men's cancers, began to expand. I believe legitimate funding sources will emerge in support of studying the survival of consciousness. But first it must be recognized as a worthy field of inquiry.

CHAPTER 21

Challenging the Media

Just as mainstream scientists are skeptical about psi phenomena, so traditional media are often skeptical. I started thinking about how the media industry engages (or not) in the topic of the afterlife. Is it fair treatment? Does it vary depending on whether it's entertainment or news? Are there any newspaper articles that are memorable for enterprise reporting on the topic of life after death? What about any films or TV programs that give credence to the idea that we live on in another form?

I remember watching Patrick Swayze and Demi Moore play a husband and wife who have a bond that survives death in *Ghost*. And I remember *Dragonfly*, in which Kevin Costner plays a grieving doctor who is contacted by his late wife through his patients' near-death experiences. That's about it for me when it comes to experiences with films' treatment of the supernatural.

I haven't been exposed to much more on TV. Years ago, I watched *Medium*, a series inspired by Allison DuBois, who claims to see people who have died. And I watched Jennifer Love Hewitt in *Ghost Whisperer*, in which she plays a woman who can see and communicate with ghosts. Again, that's about it.

In the realm of the press, I have observed a lack of serious coverage of these issues related to the survival of consciousness, whether in newspapers, broadcast news, or on the Internet.

Let me just say up front that I am biased when it comes to the press. I firmly believe in its critical importance to a functioning democracy. There's no dismissing the influence of the media. I believe that without it, we risk being uninformed. Whether the coverage focuses on presidential elections, school systems, businesses, the medical community, or cultural events, it's essential we know what's going on.

As individuals, we take this information and use it to form our opinions. We grow in our ability to reason. In short, media affect what we know, and what we know affects how we think. How we think drives our behavior and life choices.

But what about media's responsibility to readers and viewers? Yes, the news media is independent because our founding fathers decided to protect the press from government interference through the First Amendment in the Bill of Rights. But I believe the press, in turn, owes us fair and balanced coverage, given its unencumbered power and freedom.

I haven't seen that full and fair news coverage on this important issue: the question of what happens when we die.

Why is there not more coverage, and why does the coverage fail to give the topic the full respect it deserves in most cases?

In the interviews I conducted with scientists and researchers in this field, I found that they almost universally share a mistrust of the media—sadly, a mistrust they share with the public at large, according to numerous surveys. It's not hard to see why scientists feel this way. The news coverage of their field is paradoxical—good for growing some awareness but often presented in a superficial or patronizing way. As Dr. Dean Radin puts it, "The crazy thing about this field is that from the mainstream perspective, as evidenced by scientific journals, TV, and newspapers, it either doesn't exist at all, it's not considered newsworthy, or it's only suitable for silly season fodder. But when you start digging into it a bit, you find that it's much more than that. You also find that very few people are neutral about this topic—they either love it or hate it."

Dr. Charles Tart had a concern that news reports, in an attempt to appear balanced, quote people whose credentials don't match those who conducted the research. "Various media love to report on these controversies stirred up by pseudo-skeptics, and usually give the pseudo-skeptics high 'expert' status because (1) the people running a particular reporting medium are themselves pseudo-skeptical, committed to scientific materialism, (2) as cynical media people put it for decades, controversy sells more newspapers than accurate reporting, or (3) both."

I don't agree that controversy sells more newspapers than accurate reporting. Yes, conflict and drama are inherent in news. After all, safe plane landings generally aren't news; only crashes are. But accurate reporting is the essence of a quality newspaper's credibility, and no amount of sensationalism or controversy can sustain a newspaper over the long term. In my experience, reporters and editors want stories to be accurate much more than they care about whether the stories sell the newspaper.

Before actively investigating science and spirituality and reading numerous books on my journey, I really hadn't encountered any mass-circulated books dedicated to the exploration of the survival of consciousness. Nor had I read much in newspapers about scientific research on psi phenomena, either from a breaking-news standpoint or from an enterprise piece that incorporated in-depth research and analysis.

However, I think media may be evolving—slowly—in the way they approach psi phenomena. An ABC 20/20 episode hosted by Elizabeth Vargas in October 2012, titled "The Sixth Sense," offered a broad range of examples—a hodgepodge, really, which seems like a disservice to any serious exploration of a particular issue. Many of the issues were treated respectfully, although lots of corny music and jokes were included, and the timing was tied to Halloween, as if that were relevant. Ms. Vargas described the world of the paranormal as a $2 billion industry, seemingly suggesting that the money involved should make us suspicious.

The show included Theresa Caputo, the Long Island medium; Dr. Eben Alexander; Sidney Friedman, a mentalist; Laura Day, an intuitive who claims to see the future; Mattie the dog, a ghost hunter; and interestingly, Dr. Radin. Friedman failed to guess correctly when he asked Ms. Vargas to think of a number. He asked jokingly if she was impressed. She said no. For a brief two minutes at the end, Dr. Radin discussed strong evidence of precognition ability. Had he been given more time or had the format allowed for more serious conversation, the viewers would have been much better informed. Ms. Vargas did mention the Rhine Research Center, which has been doing investigations in this field for more than eighty-five years. But she casually discounted the work.

In late 2012, Katie Couric had an interesting episode she called "To Heaven and Back" on her show *Katie*. It was yet another example of blending the authentic with the questionable. The show led off with the ubiquitous Theresa Caputo. Then it introduced Colton Burpo, the little boy whose near-death experience inspired the book and now movie *Heaven Is for Real*, and Dr. Mary Neal, author of the book *To Heaven and Back*. Dr. Neal tells the story of her kayak accident in 1999 in South America and her resulting near-death experience. She also appeared on the *Today* show.

Anderson Cooper followed with his own episode called "To Heaven and Back," in which he also interviewed Mary Neal, along with Anita Moorjani, who had stage 4 lymphoma and reported a near-death experience in which she chose to return to her body.

These TV shows did not completely dismiss psi phenomena. They included a range of voices and views. In some cases they raised intriguing possibilities. But, in general, they were superficial and filled with stereotypical thinking. It was as if all weather studies—on hurricanes, tornadoes, ocean currents, droughts, rain patterns, cloud formations—were lumped into one category, and one show was planned to cover them all. Then no stories on weather studies are needed for a couple of years. I don't see how that approach is likely to yield important new knowledge for the public.

Encouragingly, the Biography Channel started a series called *I Survived . . . Beyond and Back* in 2011. It profiles personal stories of people who have passed to the other side. This was perhaps prompted by the success of *My Ghost Story*, which Biography launched in 2010, featuring stories about the paranormal by people who experienced them. The series ran for six seasons, through 2013.

Of course, television is now flowing to the Internet via YouTube. One example of informative television that can be found on YouTube is an account of the work of Dr. Melvin Morse, who studies near-death experiences in children. It includes his appearance on the Australian version of *60 Minutes*, *The Oprah Winfrey Show*, and the Public Broadcasting System of the University of Washington.

Another Internet resource is *Afterlife TV*, founded by Bob Olson and his wife, Melissa. Mr. Olson interviews a variety of experts on life after death. As a former private investigator, he attempts to separate the legitimate practitioners related to the afterlife from the phonies.

Newspapers seem to be opening up slowly to mentioning the afterlife. I was particularly taken by a Peggy Noonan column in *The Wall Street Journal* on December 27, 2011. She wrote about the eulogy that Mona Simpson had given at the funeral of Apple cofounder Steve Jobs. (Ms. Simpson is Steve Jobs's sister, and a version of her eulogy was published in *The New York Times*.) According to Noonan, "She spoke of how he looked at his children 'as if he couldn't unlock his gaze.' He'd said goodbye to her, told her of his sorrow that they wouldn't be able to be old together, 'that he was going to a better place.' In his final hours his breathing was deep, uneven, as if he were climbing. Before embarking, he'd looked at his sister Patty, then for a long time at his children, then at his life's partner, Laurene, and then over their shoulders past them. Steve's final words were: 'OH WOW. OH WOW. OH WOW.'"

Lee Hawkins, of *The Wall Street Journal*'s WSJ.com, also reported on an interesting occurrence with Whitney Houston's mother before she learned that her daughter had died. Cissy Houston was in her apartment, and her doorbell rang. When she answered it, no one was there. This was similar to what had happened to me when I would hear knocking on our front door but no one was there. And sometimes the screen door would open and close by itself. For Cissy Houston this happened several times, and finally she called downstairs to the concierge and told him someone was ringing her doorbell. He checked the security cameras and told her no one was there. She believes she was visited by Whitney's spirit because her famous daughter had promised to see her after the Grammys.

Also of interest was the front-page placement of an article in *The Wall Street Journal* on August 27, 2013, about one of the most respected bankruptcy lawyers in the country, who moonlights as a spiritual energy healer. Kenneth Klee describes himself as being able to "talk to spirits" and "mend broken bodies and souls." The article noted that there is no conclusive evidence that energy healing works, but it avoided any snickering tone.

Sadly, I could find only one legitimate documentary tackling these questions with constructive and in-depth inquiry. *What the Bleep Do We Know!? Down the Rabbit Hole* featured seventeen highly regarded professionals, including Dr. Radin, from the disciplines of physics, neurology, anesthesiology, molecular biology, spiritual healing, and journalism. But it was produced a decade ago, in 2004.

Books seem to be leading the way with serious examinations of the afterlife. In just a cursory search on Google and Amazon, I found more than eighty books on the afterlife. Happily, some were by scientists. Most were published in the last five years, a hopeful trend.

Given the immense power of those in the media establishment and their inherent ability to shape how we see the world, I am naturally interested in what might motivate them to cover the topic of life after death with more seriousness, more rigor and balance.

So I turned to someone whose broad background in media makes him as qualified as anyone I know to clarify this conundrum—my good friend Shelby Coffey. I first met Shelby when he was executive vice president and editor of *The Los Angeles Times* and I was senior vice president of advertising. There is an invisible but clearly understood line between the journalism side and the business side at quality newspapers such as *The Los Angeles Times*. Shelby and I never crossed it. We worked together for many years, and I have the highest regard and respect for him, as did all of us on the executive team that reported to our publisher at the time, Dick Schlosberg.

Shelby was the eighth editor of *The Los Angeles Times* in its 107-year history. During his tenure, the paper won five Pulitzer Prizes. Shelby previously had held editorial positions at *The Dallas Times Herald, U.S. News and World Report,* and *The Washington Post.* Shelby ultimately left *The Los Angeles Times* to join ABC News in New York as executive vice president, and then later he joined CNN as president of its business news division, replacing Lou Dobbs. In 2001 he was named a fellow of the Freedom Forum, focusing on media and First Amendment issues. He currently serves as vice chairman of the Newseum, a 250,000-square-foot museum in Washington, D.C., dedicated to news and First Amendment issues.

I asked Shelby what he thought about the way media have approached the subject of life after death. "One of the difficulties in assessing media coverage in this area is that the media is a many-headed beast," he said. "The term covers *The National Enquirer* and *The Economist, The New York Times* and Gawker, blogs and scientific journals."

And he continued: "So it's not surprising, I suppose, that we have such a bewildering variety of coverage. Some reporters and editors just avoid paranormal topics altogether. Some approach it with openness to the material, but, since the scientific community is largely skeptical, the stories often reflect that. The media will cover what they think is important. Journalists are people, and people tend to delve into the subjects that capture their passion and interest. They'll justify their time and pursue learning what they personally want to know." Fortunately, as Shelby says, "for the mainstream media the subject is often interesting—most people want to know, in the 'sleep of death, what dreams may come.'"

He then added, "And, again, we have to remember that what we call media ultimately comes down to people—reporters and editors. The deep fear of most reporters is to be taken in by a subject, to be fooled and have one's work ridiculed—especially when later revelations prove it mistaken," Shelby said. "The area of the afterlife has often attracted charlatans. So the reporter's default position is to go in on the defensive—sometimes to take a cursory glance or an easy shot."

In closing, Shelby took the topic to a different plane, one that reinforces the psychology of what occurs. He said, "In our evolutionary psychology this has an adaptive plus. Our ancestors who were suspicious often survived our potential ancestors who were too gullible. Was that new tribe coming over the hill a set of friendly traders—or a pack of killers? A lot depended on having the right answer—including who survived to become our ancestors."

It's unfortunate that this field has experienced charlatans. But it's true. I was lucky to have wasted time with only a couple myself. Ultimately, success in advancing serious awareness of this field will depend in great part on scientists. After all, let's be clear about roles. Hollywood films entertain, documentaries observe, and news media report. But scientists create. I don't mean they create facts. They create knowledge. That is why proper funding is so important. With funding comes more prolific and qualified research and believability, which, in turn, will lead to more serious coverage from the media. So scientists have their role, and so do the media.

What I hope to see is an approach where reporters maintain skepticism, which is always necessary, but seek out a broader representation of scientists doing research in this field. And when any scientist is interviewed, hopefully respect is given by the reporter, just as it would be to mainstream scientific work, regardless of the personal perspective the reporter brings to the story.

But as important a role as media can play in expanding awareness of this topic, they cannot lead. The media have tended historically to trail the general public's movement on controversial areas rather than leading the way—until news events demand coverage.

What will it take to get the media to cover this field in the right way? It will require the support of the public sentiment referred to by Abraham Lincoln's quote in the introduction of this book. The groundswell of open and pervasive public dialogue will stimulate interest among the media. When the general population, together with the scientific community, gets involved, the media will follow. In other words, when this topic legitimately goes mainstream, both in the public and in the scientific community, the media will cover it—properly.

And how do we know that is the case? Shelby says it perfectly: "The reporters who bring diligence and strong skills, skepticism and open minds, to their subjects are always the ones who get exceptional results. I am confident, as more work is done in this area, the top reporters will find surprising, maybe world-shifting, results on the frontiers of research."

CHAPTER 22

Finding My Mother

Dr. Wendland spends a great deal of time volunteering with hospice, and he has come to a provocative conclusion: "Most people are at their best when they are dying."

It reminded me of something Dr. Elisabeth Kübler-Ross once said: "The best teachers in the world are dying patients."

By early 2012 it was clear that my mother's health was slipping rapidly and that she didn't have long to live. Mentally she was as sharp as a whip. She read the newspaper from cover to cover every day and kept up with magazines and books. Though her eyesight suffered, she didn't stop pursuing her passion for reading and staying abreast of current affairs. She often pulled from Dad's library, reading books she knew he loved. She had done well coping with Dad's death over the five years since he had passed, and we as her grown children were impressed with her independence.

My relationship with Mom continued on its rocky path after Dad died, just as it had when he was alive; I maintained the routine I had been practicing for more than six decades. I had developed a foolproof method of coping with the perpetual tension between us: I simply shut her out by not really engaging with her. I would call her, and we would talk. Usually that meant she talked (very loudly), and I listened. I was polite—well, most of the time. But I didn't share my life or thoughts with her. I had long ago given up seeking or expecting real communication. I felt sorry for her and was concerned about her health issues from a distance, but nothing changed in our relationship.

At ninety-three, she was losing a lot of weight, had high blood pressure, and showed signs that her organs were giving out. She fought infections regularly and was in and out of the hospital in Dallas. My sister, Signe, lived near Mom and had been doing the heavy lifting, taking care of her appointments and managing her affairs. Signe would call me with updates, and I would listen and console her, but that was about it. I was frozen somehow. I didn't offer to come and help. I knew I was wrong, but I was too stubborn to change my old ways. No question, I was stuck in a mire of resentment, old attitudes, and grudges I'd been carrying around forever. Worse, I had absolutely no plan for how I would handle Mom's final days, which certainly would come soon. I was in a grand denial.

Jim asked me on several occasions whether I was going to visit her before it was too late. I usually changed the subject. Sometimes my guilt would set in and I would say, "Probably, but not yet." I wasn't sure it would be the best therapy for her. It would likely agitate her, and she didn't need that. I was afraid that our poor chemistry would prevent the right kind of farewell, leaving both of us with a bad memory that we would never be able to fix. So, like a child, I kept stalling, thinking the issue would go away. But the adult in me knew that if I didn't make the effort to say good-bye before she passed, there would be no second chance. How would I feel for the rest of my life to have had the choice and to have blown it?

On Sunday, March 25, 2012, as I was getting ready to take my morning walk, the lights in the bedroom closet flickered just slightly, but they clearly flickered. That had not happened in several years, and it had never happened in our new home in Florida, where we live half the year. It got my attention.

I walked to the other end of the house and asked Jim, "Did you see lights flickering?" He was reading and looked up to say, "See what?" So I just dismissed it. I thought I must have imagined it. But another part of me knew I had not.

I laced up my shoes and left the house for my daily walk. It was a spectacular day. The skies were a crystal-clear blue, and the trees had begun to blossom. The air was pristine. We were living on a small residential island where we frequently experienced the Gulf of Mexico breezes. I was at peace and enjoying the exercise when I pulled my iPhone from my pocket to check the time. It was odd. I was enjoying the serenity. Why check the time? Maybe it was habitual, but I pulled the phone out and turned it on. It was 12:44—exactly. *That's interesting,* I thought—*lights flickering for the first time in several years, and now 12:44. I better pay closer attention.*

For the past thirty-nine years since I had graduated from college, I had called my parents on Sundays. They had expected and looked forward to the ritual. After Dad died, I still called Mom on Sundays. Most of the time I dreaded the call because she had become more and more insular and was full of complaints about the assisted living facility, the other residents, her health, everything. She had become narrow in her interests in life, more negative, more critical, and unhappier.

I was reminded of something I had heard from a psychologist about what happens as we age. He said we become more of who we are, not less. Our energy to fight back the negative attributes we all possess is not as strong as we get older. So we can become more cantankerous, more irritable. I also remembered what my father had often said: "There but for the grace of God go I."

That Sunday I placed the call at about five p.m. I anticipated the usual negativism, but this Sunday was different. She was rambling, and she dropped the phone while we were talking. There was no one to help her pick it up. I could hear her struggling, but she just couldn't manage it. It was a poignant moment. It forced me to visualize her alone and helpless, and that picture brought about a visceral pain in my gut. I felt helpless too. After some minutes, all I could do was hang up. I called the assisted living facility office directly and asked them to go to her room. Then I called Signe to ask her to drive over to check on Mom. Signe had been a saint watching over Mom for the last few years. She was more patient in their relationship, and she didn't have the same personality conflict Mom and I had. Signe was far more easygoing and accepting.

When I ended the call, I turned to Jim, who was sitting next to me on the couch, and I began to cry. It was so sad—not just for my mother, but for all the elderly who are alone. As Jim held my hand and comforted me, every single one of the ceiling lights in our family room and kitchen area where we were seated began to flicker. They lit up extremely bright, then dropped down as if to go out completely. Then they went back to normal. This time Jim witnessed it in full with me. So when I said, "Did you see that?" he had no problem nodding.

I knew instantly what I had to do. I turned to him and said, "I need to go see Mom."

The next morning I made plane reservations. I had ample opportunity to reflect on my decision, and I knew with absolute certainty that I was being led to Mom. I was drawn, compelled, pulled. I didn't understand it fully at the time, but it was a very strong force that said, "You need to be with your mother before she dies." The concern that it could prove extremely difficult and painful was replaced with the knowledge that she needed me and deserved to have me there. And I wanted to be there.

So with new resolve I flew to Dallas. Signe picked me up at the airport, and we drove together to the assisted living facility. When we arrived, Mom sat up as best she could and smiled broadly. She was alert, excited, and surprisingly upbeat and warm. I thought that if I could just look past the superficial attributes that had always annoyed me, maybe I could find an intelligent, hospitable—even loving—woman.

She spoke clearly, but the stress of her age and the deterioration of her health were starkly evident. She was nearly skeleton thin and very pale. Her eyes were reflecting a soft gray instead of the more shimmering blue-green I had always known. I felt myself shiver. She was the same woman, but she was near the end, and she was suffering. Seeing her in that weakened physical state, combined with her unusually positive attitude and almost childlike vulnerability, cast a new image that nearly made me immobile.

For the rest of the afternoon, Signe and I sat together beside Mom in her bed, and we talked. She shared the experiences that had led to her life choices. Mom, like her mother before her, was a lifelong member of the Philanthropic Educational Organization (PEO), which provides educational opportunities to female students worldwide. I had been asked by the Idaho PEO to provide some information about Mom for a book they were writing. But it wasn't lost on me that I was also gathering information for her obituary.

The conversation was an easy exchange, perhaps because we had never done anything like this before. I learned things about her I'd never known—maybe because I'd never asked or hadn't really wanted to know. She spoke endearingly about growing up in Cambridge, Nebraska, with Grandma and Grandpa and how she had a childhood pony and a dog. She reflected on the days of the Dust Bowl and the Depression. She reminisced about attending Hastings College, where she met Dad. She was almost bashful talking about Dad and how they married in Cambridge in 1942 and moved to New York while he attended the seminary.

I asked her what she was doing while he was in graduate school all day. She replied that she had taught at the Ethical Culture School. I knew she'd taught second and third grade in elementary school in Cambridge, but I never knew about the Ethical Culture School. *How could I have not known that?* I wondered. She explained how she never thought twice about giving up her career as a teacher to raise the four of us. The whole conversation was almost a kaleidoscope of her life in a condensed form. It was like a review.

She had a dear friend, Pauline Walburn, whom she had known since she was five years old, in Cambridge, as well as other friends from the church in Hamilton, Ohio, where Dad had served. Many of these friends meant a lot to her, and they exchanged Christmas cards every year. She showed us her tattered address book, where thin lines, as if drawn with a ruler, crossed out the names of the many people who had died. Looking at the book, she became subdued, and I knew it was nearing time to go. She had grown tired.

Just before we left, I handed her a gift I had purchased for her in Sarasota the day before I flew to Dallas. She was not a sentimental person, nor did she seem to care much about gifts, either giving or receiving them. And it was out of character for our relationship for me to extend myself to her in this way. I don't know exactly what compelled me to go out and find this gift, but I had in my mind a picture of what I wanted for her, and I found it easily. It was a silver cross with a tiny heart charm attached to it on a dainty chain necklace. I knew Mom wasn't in a position to wear a necklace, but I had envisioned her holding it in her hands like a rosary.

I walked over to her and said, "Mom, this is for you. I want you to hold on to it and touch it whenever you're scared or lonely. When you feel it against your skin between your fingers, say a prayer and think of your family, all of us who love you, both in this world and the next. And remember your Christian faith. Think of Dad and how he's with you in spirit."

She had never had much in the way of jewelry, if any. Her life had never been about consumption or material goods. She looked at me with an almost shy expression I'd rarely seen and softly said, "Thank you."

The next day, Sunday, was a bright, sunny day. Signe and I had arranged to take Mom to lunch in her dining room, and Signe's husband, Dan, and their son, Kyle, joined us. As we sat together at a large round table, I kept looking at Mom out of the corner of my eye. She was quiet that second day. Tired. Weak. Distracted. Not all there. She struggled to keep the food on her fork and get it to her mouth. And she seemed frustrated by her body's limitations. I noticed again how feeble and thin she was. I asked myself if it was pity I was feeling or a sense of endearment. Where was the strong, argumentative, opinionated, judgmental woman I knew my whole life? Who was this quiet, retiring person who sat beside me?

After lunch, Dan and Kyle left, and Mom spoke in almost a whisper, asking if we could go outside. She was in a wheelchair, so Signe and I pushed her chair through the crowded dining room and out the front door to the long wooden porch in front of the assisted living home. She seemed revitalized by the outdoors, and the conversation flowed gently. She was having an easier time than she had at lunch, and I was relieved to see her relax. As the day warmed up, we decided to go to a covered screened-in porch, where it was a little cooler. Mom sat in her wheelchair, and Signe and I each settled into big white wicker chairs.

Time seemed suspended as I gazed at Mom, not knowing if this would be the last time I would see her. My eyes were open because my heart was open. Before me sat the woman I had known, or not known, as my mom for all these years. I felt enormous sadness and regret. But then something new, something entirely fresh, began to rise within me as my sorrow shifted to compassion, then slowly to forgiveness.

She was clutching a tattered old white purse on her lap. She carefully opened it, and when her bony and vein-ridden hand emerged, she was holding the little chain with the delicate cross and heart. I took a deep breath and a lump formed in my throat.

Mom held the gleaming cross up to the light, and as it shimmered she said, "Here's the cross you gave me, Janis. I took it to bed with me in the palm of my hand last night and held on to it. And I had it with me until you came for our lunch. I didn't want to leave it in the room, so I carried it with me in my purse that your dad gave me in Ohio when you kids were small."

Watching Mom reach into that dilapidated old purse to pull out the cherished cross and heart that I had given her provoked profound humility and affection, rare emotions from me in our relationship. Was it me changing, or her? Or was it simply a divine moment of clarity? I don't know. But I do know that it was salvation for us both.

I moved my chair closer to her and told her how much I loved her and that I had always loved her. I explained that it was just that the other things got in the way because of ego and strong personalities, coupled with a need to win Dad's affection. Then I told her about the most important gift she had given me. It was the lesson that what is important is not what happens to you, but rather how you handle what happens to you. It was a lesson I had practiced through all my struggles, especially when I lost Max.

Now it was time to give back. So I reiterated her advice.

"How you choose to handle your transition from this life to the next is what matters," I said. "You can't control what's happening to your health at ninety-three years of age. What you can control is how you handle it as you move through it. I watched you handle your grief when Dad died. You held yourself together, and you impressed all of us with your dignity and composure."

She told me what I meant to her and how very much she loved me.

Signe watched all of this and later told me that she'd never seen anything like it. She said it was almost sacred. We both felt as if there was a soft gold light in our presence. What I've concluded as I've reflected on it is that forgiveness is the greatest of all loves. And it starts when you forgive yourself.

By now the afternoon was coming to an end, and Mom was fading. As we were preparing to leave, I said, "Mom, I am convinced that everyone is waiting for you—Dad, Max, your brother George, Grandma, Grandpa, and others we know and love."

She seemed to be considering what I said. She replied, "Really, you think they're there?"

I said, "Yes, I know they are there, and they are going to welcome you. They are ready to usher you to where you need to go. You won't be alone, Mom."

We pushed her in the wheelchair back to her room. It was time to leave, and I knew this was the final good-bye for us. Mom was sitting next to her bed, and she looked up.

"Mom, remember I love you," I said.

She replied, "I love you."

Stepping out the door, I looked back one last time and said, "You are not alone, and I will join you on the other side one day."

My last memory of her is seeing her crying as we left.

Shortly after, Margaret Louise Olson, my mom, passed on.

CHAPTER 23

Reaching Out to the Other Side

One of my father's professors at Union Theological Seminary was Paul Tillich, generally regarded as a highly influential theologian and philosopher of the twentieth century. Of all Dad's professors, he was the one Dad spoke of most often, perhaps because he had delivered chapel sermons to the students. Dad had given me a copy of one of Tillich's books titled *The Courage to Be* when I was in college, and he included it again in the reading list he later provided me. For reasons I don't fully understand, after Mom died, this book came to mind. I wanted to find it and read it again. So I searched the shelves of our library and, to my amazement, I found it. There was apparently something in it for me to understand.

In *The Courage to Be*, Tillich writes about what he defines as the basic anxieties that we as individuals experience over the course of our lives. He contends that there are three: anxiety about knowing we will one day die, anxiety over the guilt we feel tied to whether we are sufficiently moral, and anxiety about whether our lives have purpose. Nestled into a comfortable chair in our living room in Sun Valley, I began rereading parts of the book. Setting it aside to reflect on its words, I found myself asking why my mother's death was different from the death of my father. Why was I feeling unsettled? I knew the answer before I finished the question. It had to do with the second of the three anxieties. I was feeling guilt about not having been a better daughter. Trying to be a good person, having a conscience, was paramount in my life, yet I had failed with my mother. I had not done the right thing for most of my life. I had let the friction overcome the love. Yes, we had reconciled at the very end, for which I was enormously grateful. But that didn't eradicate the other sixty years. Why had I been so bullheaded? Now it was too late. Or was it?

I had an idea. What if I were to have a reading with a highly respected medium to potentially connect not only with Max, but with Mom and Dad? With all three of them gone, it seemed to make sense. Would the reading confirm for me what I now suspected was true—that we live on in another form? Would Max, Mom, and Dad make their presence known? If they existed in spirit form, which I believed they did, I could work on reconnecting with Mom through prayer, meditation, or just silently talking to her once in a while.

I called Dr. Gary Schwartz, knowing he would be a good source for a quality referral, and he recommended Suzanne Giesemann. She and I corresponded by telephone and e-mail and scheduled a session at her home in Florida. We agreed that it was best if she knew very little about me other than my hope of communicating with Max and my parents.

Suzanne has an amazing background, not at all what I was expecting. She is a former navy commander who worked as a special assistant to the chief of naval operations and was selected by the chairman of the Joint Chiefs of Staff to be his aide. She was with him on 9/11 and left with him in the last plane in the air. They flew over Manhattan, looking at the burning buildings, and then flew to Washington, D.C., entering the Pentagon while it was still burning. She has flown on Air Force One with the president. She has a master's degree in national security affairs and taught political science at the U.S. Naval Academy. She was awarded the Combat Action Ribbon and the Defense Meritorious Service Medal.

When she retired from the navy after a twenty-year career, she and her husband, Ty, decided to pursue a personal goal of sailing around the world. They had sailed across the Atlantic and were in the Mediterranean when they learned that their twenty-six-year-old pregnant daughter had been struck by lightning and killed. This tragedy led Suzanne to a medium. Carefully controlling the information the medium had access to, she had an experience she describes as "incredible." During the session a young woman in her twenties who had died suddenly wanted to introduce her little boy. The child her daughter had been carrying was a boy. Suzanne knew at that moment she had to write about it.

Pursuing her interest in metaphysics, spirituality, and human empowerment, she wrote ten books on the subject, the most recent of which is *Wolf's Message*. After she began to have her own intuitive experiences, she took the intensive course at the respected Arthur Findlay College of Psychic Science in Stansted, England. She has been giving only private sessions for four years. She does not do group sessions, though she is working on developing that ability.

I was really glad Jim came with me because we drove through tornado warnings, heavy rain, and high winds as we headed to the Giesemanns' home in north-central Florida. But we made it. Suzanne warmly greeted us and made us feel very comfortable. She has a beautiful smile and bright brown eyes. She looks a lot like Dorothy Hamill, the Olympic champion figure skater. Her face is youthful and feminine, and she has the perfect posture you would expect from a navy officer. She introduced us to Ty, who is friendly and warm.

I immediately noticed the wall of books in the entryway. The Giesemanns are definitely well read. I know this because whenever Jim sees books, he can't help himself—he starts looking at the titles. Suzanne introduced us to her two well-behaved dogs, who seemed to recognize that Blue was outside in our car. She led us into her den to begin the session.

In the car driving over, Jim and I had decided that if Suzanne approved, he would start the recorder and leave the room. He was concerned that he might impact the session, as he felt he might have with Dave, the medium we'd consulted earlier. But when we walked into the den, there were three chairs. Jim said to Suzanne, "I don't want to affect the results, so I think I should leave."

Suzanne said, "No, why don't you stay? We can indicate our intention, but I have no control over who shows up. Your presence may have an impact, but that's fine."

So with Suzanne's invitation and remembering Dr. Radin's suggestion that it is sometimes helpful to have someone else in the room, Jim stayed.

As it turned out, we didn't need our recorder. Suzanne records every one of her sessions. I was her 507th reading. She's very precise. She sends a copy of the recording to her client immediately after the session. I think this is an excellent idea, speaks very highly of her, and might even be considered a requirement for selecting a qualified medium.

Suzanne asked if we could start the session with a prayer to center her. This is sacred work to her. We held hands, and she prayed:

"Oh, God, the great spirit and the spirit world, my helpers on the other side, thank you for this opportunity to sit with Janis and Jim and to serve you. I am so awed and grateful to be chosen for this work. May I be worthy of it today. May those on the other side come through with incredible clarity. I am so grateful for the answered prayers and the way things have been going, and may they continue and continue to expand. I'll do my best to apply all of your teachings today, and we'll fill this room with love to match your vibration. And thank you for the best possible outcome."

As we began the session, Suzanne closed her eyes, breathed deeply through pursed lips, and twitched her mouth from side to side. She looked up at us and said, "I can't help this twitching. Gary Schwartz told me I look ridiculous, and I know it does, but that's my guide—that helps. It's definitely giving me a sign that he's here."

She didn't look ridiculous at all. It's the way I would expect someone to look if she was intensely trying to communicate with the spirit world. At first it wasn't clear what she meant when she said, "He's here." *Who?* I wondered. She had already told us she couldn't control who showed up. Soon we learned it was more than just one "he" that would show up. As the session proceeded, we had four spirits make their presence known—Max, my dad and mom, and Jim's dad.

It wasn't foolproof, but we slowly learned to tell which one she was communicating with by the direction Suzanne's head was facing. It was as if she were seated at a round table of guests, with her head facing the person she was speaking to. As her head turned in different directions, it was an indication that a different spirit was communicating. She said she was drawn to the side when the communicating spirit is a mother or father and to the center when it is a nonblood relative such as a husband, partner, or friend. She spoke with the spirits, often asking them to give more. They came intermittently, not sequentially, so her head was moving from side to side. Most of the time her eyes were closed. She says it helps her concentrate, and she wants to avoid feedback from her clients.

Now and then she would ask me if something she said made sense. I think it was a way of fine-tuning her interpretation. Suzanne said she gains access to the spirit world by listening to a voice that she hears within herself. She also receives images and symbols. But she hears more than anything else. She is very clairaudient, as opposed to clairvoyant, which involves sight.

Sometimes I tried to be helpful, and she would say, "No, don't tell me." She didn't want to be led in any way. She was very independent.

She began our session by telling me about Max. She felt his presence as a kind of weakness or physical collapse. She said the "feeling of collapse" is generally what she experiences when there is a physical illness, not an accident. This is consistent with how Max died. She said she thought he had "a cancerous condition" and was pointing to the abdomen or stomach. She said she thought it ultimately led to metastasis of the lymph nodes. Of all the ways someone can die, Suzanne had narrowed it not only to cancer, but also to the area of the body where the cancer resided. The esophagus connects to the stomach, so while it wasn't 100 percent correct, it was extremely close. And Max's cancer had metastasized to his lymph nodes, which is what ultimately made his cancer fatal.

When it came to how she defined his personality, I thought it interesting that she could have chosen any number of attributes, but she chose "a patient man, it would take a lot to ruffle him" and said that Max would "examine things" before he reacted. This was absolutely characteristic of him. She said he possessed an "inner calm and knowing about things," which is also true. He didn't seek to join others or to be accepted by them, either. He was happy as a loner quietly reading his books and learning. She described a "deep sacredness" in Max that she would not call a "religion," however. She said he was drawn to this path of what he considered sacred, though again, not from a religious standpoint. She's right about this too. Max believed books, music, and art were sacred. He believed the pursuit of learning was sacred. He once said that the closest he felt to "knowing" God was when he was in the presence of a great book.

Suzanne also said Max wasn't comfortable with conflict, that "his reaction would be to withdraw, or go in a room and shut the door." I remember the few times I came home from a bad day, feeling like a "crank ball" in the mood for a fight. But even though I tried to stoke the flames of an argument, Max retreated. It wasn't his thing. I found this frustrating since I liked a good fight now and then. I couldn't have one at work, so why not at home occasionally? I learned over the four years we were married that if I was going to fight, it would be with myself.

The closest we ever came to a battle was a time I didn't even mean to start one. It was a lazy Saturday afternoon, Max was at the gym, and I came up with the brilliant idea of rearranging the books on the shelves in our library. What I failed to realize were two rather significant things. One, 90 percent of the books were Max's, and two, he had alphabetized them by author's last name. Not being aware, I rearranged the books according to color and size, a method I perceived to be much more aesthetically appealing. I was quite proud of my accomplishment.

When Max came home later that afternoon, I heard him in the library making a kind of huffing noise from his nose. I walked in to see if he was okay and to ask if he noticed how pretty the book display was. Max was leaning down, picking up a large, heavy art book from the neatly stacked pile I'd made of all the same-size books on the very bottom shelves. He turned around slowly, and his face was the color of a tomato.

"What's wrong?" I asked.

"You didn't rearrange my books, did you?" he asked in a John Wayne kind of voice.

"Well...yes, I did," I squeaked out in a Minnie Mouse voice.

"How many?" he asked.

"Well...kind of...all of them...sort of," I said.

He asked me not to do that again, and it was over. That night was not the most fun night I've ever had. It was quiet, and he retreated. But I learned my lesson about the books. That was never going to happen again!

But back to our session with Suzanne. She told me Max was "liberal, a Democrat, and that he was on the phone a lot— maybe two phones at a time. He was fair with the people he worked with, but exacting." She said she saw him "in his office and a desk covered with papers." Again, all true. Max was a "by the book" Democrat. And Max was not a computer person. He was a yellow-lined-legal-pad person.

She said Max was meticulous—"I see socks lined up in a drawer and rolled just right...shoelaces and double knotting his laces...suits lined up but very neat and very careful." This was fascinating to me because it was quintessential Max. Just like his CD collection and his books, his socks, shoes, and suits were organized with precision and according to a plan. And the bulk of his dress shoes had laces. They weren't loafers. Too casual for Max.

There were other things Suzanne said about Max that weren't wholly accurate. But they were in the minority. She had done an outstanding job defining Max overall.

With Dad, it was a mixed bag between what I considered to be accurate and what wasn't. For example, she thought Dad had a heart issue, but it was cancer that took his life. And she mentioned a problem with his leg requiring a cane. This made no sense. She also thought he had engineering and research in his background, which he didn't. And she thought he was cantankerous, which he wasn't, except maybe at the end of his life.

But she was correct about describing his humble beginnings and his rise to a "higher" life through his service in the ministry. She also articulated his love for my mother perfectly and elaborated on how strong their marriage was. She talked about how he liked to tell jokes. This was true. When I was growing up, humor was big in our home. She said Dad was proud of me and wanted to "envelop" me in a hug. That sounded like him, although it was generic.

I was eager to know what she would convey from Mom. Suzanne said that Mom was "somebody that just would have been not real pleasant with their words." Totally true. She said she was experiencing Mom as telling me "what to do, how to behave, what to be like." That was certainly correct. "She is very judgmental," explained Suzanne. "You were always walking on eggshells, not sure how to behave around her. She was unpredictable." It was uncannily accurate.

Then Suzanne said something very illuminating. She said, "What I'm feeling is somebody who was in their own little world."

It struck home. Had Mom been in her own world all those years while I was in mine? Is that why we didn't connect? Couldn't connect? While I was feeling that she was being judgmental of me, was she feeling the same about me because I was in fact judging her? Was I expecting her to be what I wanted her to be instead of allowing her to be who she was—someone in her own world, a world I could never know? Was she teaching me from another realm that love isn't dependent on being alike? Was I learning that love doesn't judge; love accepts?

Here's the important thing. I didn't need to feel guilty and neither did she. We both had played a role in the relationship we shared. I thought of that special moment on the porch in Dallas with Mom and Signe. We extended ourselves to each other, and we finally connected. The truth of our love and the power of forgiveness were indisputable. If she or I was guilty of anything, it was of being imperfect, which is to say we were guilty of being human.

I believe it was love and forgiveness that prompted Jim's dad's visit as well. Suzanne said that there was a spirit with a military connection who had entered the space. (Jim's dad was a career officer in the air force.) She said this spirit was a man and that she "could just cry right now, the emotion is so strong." She defined his personality and career perfectly. She was very specific. In fact, the message was so detailed that, turning to Jim, I could see he was literally stunned. Suzanne said Jim's dad was there to apologize for what had been a turbulent relationship between the two of them. She said he took responsibility and wanted to tell Jim, "You're a bigger man than I was. You have a huge heart." I looked at Jim. He had tears in his eyes. I've only seen him cry one other time—at the funeral for his mother.

As impressive as all this was, there were two things so exceptional, so extraordinary, they not only sealed my belief in Suzanne and her ability to connect to the spirit world; they served to prove to me that the spirit world exists and exists right here alongside us.

At one particular moment in the session, Suzanne looked at me and said, "What I'm hearing is, I heard Dirty Harry and then it took me to Sacramento. I don't know why. Any idea, any link, does that make sense? Dirty Harry is Clint Eastwood. Clint Eastwood was the mayor in Carmel. Right?"

I was completely blown away. This was so obscure, so singular, there is no way it could be anything but authentic.

Max and his partners at Townsend Raimundo Besler & Usher in Sacramento helped pass a ballot initiative in Monterey County for the Pebble Beach Company in 2000. Part of the measure approved the construction of a new golf course. The partners, including Max, met and worked with Clint Eastwood. What are the odds that Suzanne, who did not know me, Max, or anything about us, would know this?

But what really took my breath away and brought tears to my eyes was when Suzanne said, "I'm seeing a man laid out in a coffin with his hands across his chest and flowers in his hands. I know that doesn't make sense for a man, but I'll just tell you that's what I see. He's talking about the stars, the stars in the sky, and he's pointing up at one."

At Max's funeral service, after Tanner and I finished delivering our eulogies from the pulpit, we walked down the steps, and we each placed a white tulip on top of the coffin. Soon after, the Reverend Jesse Vaughan walked to the pulpit and read the homily he had prepared for the service. It included an excerpt from *The Little Prince* that I believe he had selected especially to comfort Tanner. I clung to the words as my heart broke, not just for me but also for my son. Feeling Tanner's shoulder softly pressed against mine as we sat in the pew, I knew that if Max were whispering from the heavens through the stars, he would choose laughter as the way for Tanner to keep him in his heart forever.

All men have stars, but they are not the same things
for different people. For some, who are travelers, the
stars are guides. For others they are no more than little
lights in the sky. For others, who are scholars, they are
problems . . . But all these stars are silent. You—You alone
will have stars as no one else has them. . . . In one of
them I shall be laughing . . . And you will sometimes open
your window, so, for that pleasure . . .

Antoine de Saint-Exupéry,
The Little Prince

CHAPTER 24

Finding Myself

When Dad passed on in 2007, we honored his request to be cremated, and his ashes were held at the Lockenour-Jones Mortuary in Cambridge, Nebraska. He and Mom had asked that they be buried at the same time in Cambridge, where Mom had grown up and where her parents and grandparents were buried at Fairview Cemetery. A joint plot had been reserved for Mom and Dad next to her ancestors in the Thorndike family plot.

So after Mom's passing in April 2012, we arranged for the two of them to be buried next to each other as they'd wished. We requested a joint headstone to mark their place. Written across the front were words chosen by my sister-in-law Marky: TOGETHER 70 YEARS—AND FOREVER. We placed a PEO marker, indicating her membership in the Philanthropic Educational Organization, on the stone to honor Mom's many years as a member.

In late August, our family was able to come together for a memorial service in my parents' honor. Cambridge, with a population of 1,063, is not easy to get to. It means flying into Omaha and then driving four hours west to Cambridge. With family members coming from different parts of the country, it took awhile for us to organize our schedules to be there at the same time.

Jim and I arrived late afternoon on Thursday. We had driven our faithful Toyota Sequoia from Sun Valley, Idaho, because it was easier than flying, and we could bring along Blue the Wonder Dog and his Frisbee collection. I hadn't been to Cambridge since visiting my parents in 2003, when they lived there briefly in their mideighties. I had forgotten that it had only one restaurant, Town Talk, open for dinner. Jim apparently wasn't clear just how tiny this town was. After we sat down at a small table with a red-and-white-checkered cloth, he asked for the wine list. A waitress with rumpled hair, looking to be straight out of 1960, stared at him as if he were from Mars and said in a completely deadpan voice, "Honey, we haven't had a wine list for fifteen years."

The next day, Marky and my brother Kurt arrived as did my sister, Signe, with her husband, Dan. My other brother, Brian, arrived from Connecticut with his son, Jason. I was very happy to see Jason, as he has a wry sense of humor and is a kindhearted person. I enjoy his company, and it was comforting to have a representative of the next generation among us. Tanner had been unable to come because he was in the first week of his new job after having graduated from college.

We all stayed at Cambridge Bed and Breakfast, a beautiful converted home on the National Register of Historic Places. The owner, Gloria Hilton, and her husband, Gerald, are fourth-generation residents of the area. Gloria, like my Mom, belonged to PEO, and she and Mom were friends. She was a delightful hostess and, with the help of her family, served us some delectable meals while we were there. They took us in as if we were their own family.

On Friday night, after everyone had arrived, we went out to dinner together at Town Talk. Jim did not ask for the wine list, but he got one anyway. The waitress from the night before recognized him as we came in and, after a few minutes, sauntered over to our table. With a sly smile, she passed a small sheet from her green order pad to Jim. She had written in pencil, "Wine list: Red. White. Blush." Jim made an "I deserve it" face, and the rest of us had a hearty laugh. It turned out to be an enchanted evening, as we caught up on our lives and relived stories we'd all told before. It had been four years since we were last together at my wedding to Jim in Sun Valley. Flickering in the recesses of my mind was a thought about how many more times we would be together before one of us was gone. If only we could hold these moments longer.

The memorial service was the following morning, Saturday. We had decided to include only our family. Mom had been very clear that she wanted a religious service at Trinity United Methodist Church, where she and Dad had been married seventy years earlier. The pastor, a soft-spoken woman named Sherry Sklenar, conducted the service. Each of the sons and daughters had written a brief eulogy.

I started mine with, "Today I will speak directly to Mom and Dad because I truly believe they are present in spirit." These are words I would never have spoken in 2004, when Max died. I had not anticipated the influence he was to have on me. Remarkably, I had known him longer in death than in life.

Now absorbing the death of my parents, I had a sense of peacefulness, and it was for both of them. I didn't know all the answers, but I accepted the reality of Mom's and Dad's deaths with an emotional and mental calmness. I knew in my heart that they were present because I knew that love never dies.

And there was more that Max had taught me. Stirred by the music, the reverence within the church, and the warmth of my family seated together, I had an insight. It had to do with hope and free will.

The journey I had been on was emboldened by hope. Who can measure the value of hope? It's infinite. Hope drove my ambition to learn, to seek out understanding and knowledge. Further, I recognized this precious hope was born of free will, the free will Dr. Wendland had talked about, the free will we all possess as humans. Each one of us decides if we're hopeful or despairing, if we believe or do not believe in life beyond death. Whatever choice we make, it isn't something that's dictated or handed down. It is self-developed, making it all the more powerful. Because I made the conscious decision to hope that there was more, I set aside distrust and fear and opened up to the unknown.

Glancing at my family, I was struck again by the tug in my heart that I had felt the night before when I realized that, except for Jason, we had all reached the age where we are facing our own mortality. I studied the faces of Jim, of my family, lingering longer than normal to freeze their expressions in my memory. I had an overwhelming sense of how very much I loved each one of them and how grateful I was to have them in my life.

Thanks to the beautiful eulogies Kurt, Brian, and Signe gave as well as the words of Pastor Sklenar, the service was meaningful and memorable. I am sure Mom and Dad were pleased. But the whole time I couldn't shake a pervading thought. It had to do with Max. I was celebrating the lives of two of the most important people in my life, in a place strongly tied to me, to them, to generations of my family on both sides. Yet it was Max—far removed from my Nebraska heritage—who had taught me how to understand the death of my father and, even more surprising, that of my mother, someone I had never understood in life. Just as my mother's lesson about how we deal with adversity had helped me through Max's death, Max's lessons had helped me through my parents' deaths. And he had given me this gift from an even more remote place, the other side.

So where was Max on this important day? I had learned from him to pay attention. Because of him I knew that the spirits of the departed are always close. He taught me that it's possible to connect beyond the grave, that love trumps geography, time, and space. But I was not hearing from him that day. I wondered why.

After the service, we had lunch at the B and B, then went for a walk through town, recalling memories of visits when we were kids. I remember so well my grandpa's store, now called Thorndike Hall, the place where big-band leader Glenn Miller played. We headed over to the beautifully landscaped park where Grandpa had managed to put on some awesome home-grown fireworks shows for the Fourth of July when we were kids. We would sit at big wooden picnic tables eating hamburgers and cucumbers with onions while the smell of charcoal filled the air. Grandpa would fuss with his bag of fireworks while we pranced around with our skinny gold fireworks sparklers. Being together again with my two brothers and sister in a place we'd been together fifty years ago held precious meaning. I felt that same swelling in my heart that I'd felt over dinner at Town

Talk and in the church during the service. And remaining just underneath it was a sliver of anxiety about Max's absence. Why wasn't I feeling his presence?

The next morning I was very sad as we said our good-byes. We shared all the usual "You'll have to come and visit" and "We'll see each other soon" promises, but I suspected there was a reason my heart was pounding just slightly. I worried that with our busy lives, it wouldn't be soon enough.

I decided I needed some time with nature to reflect on these past few days. While Jim packed the car, Blue and I went for a walk. It was a glorious day. I took yesterday's route through the center of town, where little has changed over the century, then made my way to the park again. Cambridge is on the Republican River and Medicine Creek, and I knew the park to be characteristic of a community that looks after its environment. I began reminiscing about swimming in the pool there with Kurt and Brian fifty years earlier. I entered the park and discovered a meticulously manicured walking-trail system. Blue and I followed it and ended up next to the gurgling, crystal-clear creek.

Suddenly I saw before me a walking bridge. Boldly embossed on a plaque were the words: THE MAX BRIDGE. I stopped in my tracks. What was this doing here? It wasn't here the last time I was in Cambridge. I found myself asking the old familiar question: Is this a coincidence? I know Max is not an uncommon name, but still, what are the chances? Naturally, I couldn't help thinking that a bridge goes from here—to there. What a metaphor. And I remembered Traci Ireland telling me that Max needed to cross "the bridge." I rushed back to tell Jim the news. Max wasn't missing after all.

As Jim and I were leaving town, we stopped by the assisted living facility to visit Pauline Walburn, Mom's best friend. This required that we leave Cambridge by a different route than we took when we arrived two days earlier (there are only two). About a mile out of town as we headed west, we saw a large industrial sign posted prominently alongside the road. It read BESLER INDUSTRIES. What was Max's last name doing on a sign outside the only manufacturing plant in Cambridge? According to the White Pages, there are only 750 people named Besler in the United States. So this struck me as very unusual.

Ultimately, I viewed both the Max Bridge and the Besler Industries sign as synchronicity. They were messages from Max and the spirit world that our connections with loved ones are not limited by place. I believe that my grandparents, my parents, and Max have been united in the afterlife. And they wanted to make sure I knew it.

I am humbled and grateful for my journey. I am convinced that Max and the spirit world have been guiding me throughout this time and remain present today. And I don't think I am special. I believe each of us has the potential to experience the soft edges between this life and the next. What we see will vary on a spectrum, but it's there if we open our eyes and hearts and pay attention. My story is unique, but, paradoxically, it is also universal.

The Hand on the Mirror is about possibility in our lives. It's about the bridge from this world to the next. And as much as anything, this book and my own spiritual journey are about love. We are all one thing, bound by love.

I still get messages from Max—but fewer of them. The number 12:44 shows up at significant times, and lights flicker with no obvious cause when something important is about to happen. I've chosen to believe that when the lights flicker, it's Max winking at me. Unlike a smile, a wink is far more intimate. The connection is personal. I don't go out of my way looking for signs from Max, but I remain open when it happens. I have moved on and am living my life with Jim, fulfilled by all that it has to offer.

I regularly visit with Tanner in San Francisco. One recent Saturday, he and I were walking on Powell Street near Union Square when we heard the clanks and clatters of a passing cable car, its winding wheels gliding through the tracks. Turning to watch it, I asked Tanner if he remembered the time he, Max, and I had caught a cable car years earlier. Tanner would have been around ten years old. It was a crisp autumn Saturday, and the three of us had just toured Alcatraz and were making our way back for an early dinner near Union Square. We heard the clanging of the cable car bell and the whirring of the cables beneath and turned to watch it pass. Just then the car stopped and Max said, "Let's jump on! Why not?" Quickly we hoisted ourselves up onto the trolley, and away we went, snuggled close to one another inside the already too-crowded car. The breeze off the bay hit our faces, and we huddled tighter. Max put his arms around the two of us, and time stopped. The moment was perfection. That memory and others like it are how Max lives on inside both Tanner and me and will for the rest of our lives.

Not too long ago, Jim, Blue, and I took one of our famous road trips and headed for the West Coast. We stopped in Sacramento to visit friends, including my former housekeeper Helen. Jim, Helen, and I had lunch at a favorite local Greek restaurant. I hadn't seen Helen for a while, and it felt great to catch up with her life and the lives of her family members. I was gratified to hear that she continues to believe, as I do, that Max kept his promise. We agreed it was he who came back to let us know there was more, just as he said he would.

On the day we buried my parents' ashes in Cambridge, Nebraska, atop the gentle rolling hills of the cemetery at the edge of town, I was overwhelmed by a realization, finding such clarity in that moment. As I stood quietly among the maple and fir trees, I knew that I was a different person than the woman who stood by Max's grave in Yountville, California, eight years earlier. My safe, predictable, and relatively controlled life, the one that gave me security and continuity, had become unhinged. I was faced with extraordinary experiences that changed my way of looking at the world. Since Max's death, I had morphed from grief, to fear, then to amazement, and finally to a curiosity and hope that sparked a pilgrimage. I ultimately arrived at a more complex view of life and death. I am a much deeper person now, capable of more profound emotions. And I am better prepared for my own mortality and all that it entails.

In other words, death taught me about life. I rarely waste time anymore. There's less squabbling, and I don't judge those I love who choose to be different. I don't get distracted during the coveted times I have with family and friends. I live in the present, acutely aware of paying attention to all dimensions. I relish the brief glimpses into the mysteries of our existence. The hand on the mirror that was revealed to me changed everything.

Afterword

That's my story. My dream that I could share it openly, formulated on the beach in Bodega Bay, California, has been realized. Now I am hoping you will share your stories. My website, http://thehandonthemirror.org, has been designed to provide a framework for you to do just that. Please log on and join the conversation. Help us build the public sentiment that Abraham Lincoln reminded us that we need in order to succeed.

Acknowledgments

The Hand on the Mirror would not exist without the helping hands of others.

First and foremost I want to thank Mary Evans, my literary agent. Mary believed in me and was able to quickly find others who shared in that belief.

I'd like to thank the exceptional people at Grand Central Publishing, especially my editor, Deb Futter. Deb's support and passion for this book made it a reality. I also want to thank Jamie Raab, Brian McLendon, Matthew Ballast, Jimmy Franco, Oscar Stern, Dianne Choie, and Elizabeth Kulhanek.

In addition, I want to thank the researchers, scientists, academics, and spiritual practitioners I interviewed. Without them, this book would not have been possible. Thanks go to Dr. Paul Wendland, Dr. Dean Radin, Dr. Bruce Greyson, Dr. Gary Schwartz, Dr. Carol de la Herran, Dr. Charles Tart, Dr. Robin Van Doren, Loyd Auerbach, Stephen Barr, Traci Ireland, Dave Campbell, and Suzanne Giesemann. I would also like to thank Bob and Phran Ginsberg, Lynn Dickerson, and Shelby Coffey for their contributions.

I want to express my deep gratitude to my friend Carol

Acknowledgments

Hanner. As a former newspaper editor, Carol's skill in editing my manuscript and helping me prepare it for submission to Grand Central Publishing was invaluable.

I am forever grateful to the two men I love most in life, Jim and Tanner. Jim not only supported me, he joined me on my journey. Tanner never doubted me and kept me rooted during the hardest days of my life. The two of them were like the warm golden glow of a lantern lighting the path along the way. Without the light, there would have been no path, and without the path, no journey. I owe them everything.

Finally, I want to thank Max, who initially inspired this journey and taught me, before and after his passing, about the limitless nature of love.